D1596438

Born a Hunter

Born a Hunter

Dwight Van Brunt

Published by
SPORTING CLASSICS

Born a Hunter
Published by Sporting Classics.

Copyright ©2009 by Dwight Van Brunt

Publisher: Chuck Wechsler

Editor: Matt Coffey

Art Director: Ryan Stalvey

Graphic Designer: Chris Nye

Illustrations: Jocelyn Russell

Printed in the United States.

First Edition

Library of Congress Control Number: 2009924830

ISBN 978-0-9794853-8-1

Dedication

To Jamy Traut for hanging the African moon, Dave Leonard for sharing his Alaska, and to my family – Kellie, Ross & Keni.

About the Artist

Raised in the Rocky Mountains of Colorado, Jocelyn Russell discovered her passion for art at an early age. Being part of a family that spent every possible moment outdoors, she developed an intense interest in wildlife and began recording her impressions on canvas. Her natural ability to capture color and motion gained a loyal following, allowing Jocelyn to became a full-time wildlife artist nearly 20 years ago. Since then, the success of her work in paint, bronze and jewelry has given her the opportunity to travel the world and photograph animals for study.

Jocelyn's art has gained international recognition and earned important awards, including being twice-named Featured Artist by the Rocky Mountain Elk Foundation, as well as Sponsor Artist for Colorado Ducks Unlimited. Always one to give back, she has contributed countless works to support the fund-raising activities of wildlife conservation groups.

For *Born a Hunter,* Jocelyn created an oil painting of the author's Cape buffalo for the trade edition dust jacket, as well as original graphite sketches for each chapter. She also sketched the Cape buffalo bust for the cover of the deluxe edition.

Jocelyn Russell works from her studio on Washington's San Juan Island. The original sketches from *Born a Hunter*, as well as other works in paint and bronze, are available at www.wildlifebronzes.com.

Jocelyn Russell
© 2009

Contents

Jacelyn Russell
© 2009

Contents

Jocelyn Russell
© 2009

Foreword

Having some experience in these matters, what I tell prospective book writers is that they're in for an awful lot of work, and in the limited marketplace of folks like you and me who love to hunt and love to read about it, they aren't going to get rich.

I'm pretty sure this is what I told my old friend Dwight Van Brunt late one Arctic twilight while we were chasing sleep – after having chased, rather than counted, sheep through a long, foot-blistering day – somewhere in the Yukon's Pelly Mountains. Of course, I didn't expect him to pay any attention. Hunters are compelled to hunt, hence the title of this book. This is more than part of who we are; it's part of what we are. If you're reading these lines, you understand. Equally compelling, though perhaps even more incomprehensible, writers must write. Knowing that Dwight had that strange compulsion, I expected him to ignore me.

For those of us who love to hunt and love to read about it, this is a very good thing. In fact, it's a wonderful thing when that vexing compulsion to spill out words, whether on Hemingway's foolscap tablets, Ruark's battered typewriter or today's laptops, coincides with a genuine story to tell. The good news is that Dwight does indeed have a story to tell, and he tells it well.

Dwight Van Brunt is having a remarkable hunting career. I use the present tense, because it isn't over. Personally, I consider this exceptionally fortuitous, because Dwight is a bit younger than I am, and I certainly don't consider my own hunting nearing the end! But we've shared some great adventures, and we've each had some great adventures separately, and it's fair to say that we go back a long, long ways.

Thirty years, to be exact. Back in 1979, before I joined Petersen Publishing Company, I was freelance writing and doing some work as a hunting consultant. I received, and replied to, an inquiry from a young Dwight Van Brunt, asking about a caribou hunt for him and his dad. I'm pretty sure they didn't book, but that isn't surprising, since I'm not much of a salesman!

A couple more years passed, and when I was the editor at *Petersen's Hunting* magazine, I purchased a story on a handgun hunt for mountain goat, written by the same Dwight Van Brunt. To some extent this is all my fault, but at the time I didn't know it. Only in the necessary preparation for this Foreword did I learn that this was the first story Dwight had ever sold. So having assumed my rightful role as Dr. Frankenstein, I was totally out of order in attempting to discourage my creation . . . but it mattered little, because he wasn't about to listen!

Through successive iterations of his career, in our industry Dwight has become known as a marketing icon – but he has continued to follow his compulsions as both hunter and writer. I am fortunate that our paths have crossed in many wonderful places. The first time we hunted together was on a pronghorn hunt on the Fort Belknap Indian Reservation in Montana. Not once but twice we hunted Arctic grizzly in Alaska with Dave Leonard, and both of those were difficult situations. I was the "designated writer" and Dwight was the "industry host." No matter how hard I tried I couldn't get my friend to take the first shot. On the first hunt neither of us scored, and with the spring heating up too quickly, the plane he had just vacated broke through the ice at Kotzebue and sank in the icy water! On the second attempt I got a wonderful bear . . . and Dwight did not.

He did a little better when we hunted together in Sonora. You'll read about that later. My desert mule deer was okay. His was spectacular. On that Yukon hunt, when I gently tried to dissuade him from writing this book, his ram was better than mine – but my feet were a lot better than his. But Dwight is a driven hunter and on those terrible feet he went forth and took a beautiful ram. You will also read about his marvelous success in making hunters of his son, Ross, and his daughter, Keni. This, of course, is the most important legacy of a man who was "Born a Hunter" – and compelled to write about it. This is Dwight's first book, but I'm sure there will be others, and we all will be more enriched.

Craig Boddington
Paso Robles, California
November 14, 2008

Introduction

The title of this book is no accident. I was born a hunter. Other than family, hunting the world's great game is the only thing that has ever held more than passing interest. Chances are you feel much the same, else you would not be reading these words. To my mind, that we are hunters makes us very fortunate.

My father is a hunter. Some of my most treasured memories are of following him through the central Washington sage, his brace of magical dogs searching out quail, chukar and the odd pheasant that almost always fell to his J.C. Higgins shotgun. Dad always found a way to make me feel part of every hunt – that the birds taken were equally his and mine – and drove the point home by letting me carry the roosters, tailfeathers extending from the pocket of my much-too-big vest. He taught me how to shoot, and at his side I took my first birds and deer. Years later, when he was crowding 70, we climbed a Montana mountain where he shot his only elk. Those spike-horns are worth more to me than all the gold in Fort Knox.

My son and daughter are hunters, lucky to have grown up in Montana and luckier still to have hunted Africa in their teens. This passion has served them well, whether measured by how it helped them navigate the challenges of life or by the trophies they have nailed to their walls.

This book is the product of a youthful dream that refused to pass. I learned to read at a very young age by following along as my parents and maternal grandmother read aloud, or more than likely recited by memory, stories from the pages of hunting magazines stacked about the house. Pursuing that dream led to a career in the outdoor industry, allowing me to share campfires with some of the heroes of my youth and to work both for and with many exceptional and like-minded people. These associations rekindled a desire from long ago: to write about the hunts I have been so fortunate to experience. I sincerely hope you enjoy them.

Dwight Van Brunt
Kalispell, Montana
May 25, 2009

Jocelyn Russell
© 2009

Chapter 1

Tendril of a Hunter's Dream

It seems that a traveled hunter will eventually develop an obsession for a single species, forsaking all others. Likely transient, the interest may change with age or opportunity or more probably following eventual success, but the intensity it brings is unrelenting. The afflicted find themselves sitting the board of the namesake conservation organization, searching for second copies of obscure hunting books that mention their critter and walking the aisles of sport shows with hopes of finding the outfitter or professional hunter that can finally, Scout's honor, take them to the secret mountain or valley or thicket where their one and only is waiting. These hunts are booked three years in advance following consideration usually reserved for the selection of a second wife, and the thrill of writing the deposit check is akin to the birth of a son.

A visit to the home or office of one so inclined leaves little doubt to their leaning. Mailboxes, entry gates and doors are adorned with the graven image. Parked in the driveway are cars and trucks wearing license plates personalized with a related reference like SLVRTIP or 100PNDR or SPRLHRN or GRNDSLM. Inside is a shrine of bronze and paint and special rifles for specialized uses that were somehow justified but cannot be explained to anyone who has not suffered under similar circumstance. If married and still on good general terms, the lady of the house will likely be draped in jewelry or clothing or set the table with plates and crystal and napkin holders that pay unwitting homage.

For most hunters, the dream of dreams will never become reality. Consider, for instance, the number of double rifles and heavy bolt guns wearing rib-mounted, 3-leaf irons under possession of nearsighted deer hunters with elephant dreams. Most of these rifles will never be fired and many do not even have ammunition in proximity. These big bore owners are the same stalwarts who will slur an old friend who shows up for a Saturday morning deer hunt as a damn fool for bringing his new bolt-action wonder-cannon that weighs less than a sack lunch and shoots flat out to four miles as being over-gunned, impractical and possibly a showoff. They throw these observations knowing the nearest they will ever come to Africa is the southeast corner of the back yard. And so it goes.

Those who claim to know about such things council that the proper first step in dealing with a life-encompassing distraction is admission. The remaining 11 steps, they say, are effortless by comparison. While it is prudent to regard those who give advice with suspicion, especially if doing so is their chosen profession, they may be right in this instance, even though taking out a mortgage to book the hunt may be closer to the healing hand.

The bug that bit me was kudu. It bit hard, too, and a long time ago, chewing its way into mind and life through books and magazine articles back when my first baseball glove still fit and girls were a noisy nuisance. I became a deer hunter then an elk hunter, even made it to Alaska several times before the chance to scratch the itch came along. Then one morning the phone rang and I was going to Africa.

The caller was an old friend. He spoke about places we would go and who would be the other members of our party – all first-rate. The food, the scenery, the side trips, the background of the professional hunter all came dribbling out while I waited for the list. I didn't care if we were going without food and water, wearing hoods like hostages or taking possession of King Solomon's mines, the list of what we would hunt was all that mattered. Finally it came. The rest of the details were lost, but the trip would end on a Namibian ranch with two days dedicated to kudu. Friend though he is, he tortured me unknowingly by mentioning kudu last.

We landed in South Africa some months later, connected with the PH and drove to a game-rich private ranch where we would spend the next few days. I don't recall ever eating better or laughing harder or seeing brighter stars than we did while on that ranch. The first days brought springbok and gemsbok, followed by duikers, assorted varmints and even a great morning of duck hunting if there is such a thing. Everyone shot well. Two of us made a successful side trip to the Kalahari for eland, perhaps the finest hunting day of our lives, then it was off to Namibia for kudu.

We drove 16 hours straight, arriving in time to hunt the last, best hour. Two days plus that hour didn't seem like enough, but we spotted a bull within minutes. Actually, the PH spotted him and told me to shoot. The rut was on. I saw a cow, not the bull, because I didn't realize that the cow I was looking at was the bull and that bulls lay those wonderful, twisting horns along their back and fittingly look down their nose at intruding hunters before disappearing into the brush. I didn't see his horns until it was too late. They were big.

Early the next morning we spotted him or maybe his twin moving away with a young bull and five cows in tow. We followed the tracker following them, catching up as the sun topped the horizon. Not far now, we could see the nearly white bars running down their sides and hear an occasional soft crunch when a hoof pushed down on a rock. A cow moved toward an opening that for an instant would allow a clear shot. Others followed.

I took a knee and pushed the wing safety away. The resident PH crouched just behind, whispering unnecessary instructions.

The bull stepped into the opening, the PH whispered, "Shoot!" and the bull crumpled. Then the tracker said something in an unpromising tone.

The PH apologized. "I told you to shoot the wrong bull," I heard him say through a gathering fog. "The bulls switched places and I did not notice in time to stop your shot. We will take the meat and keep hunting. You have another bull on your license and plenty of time."

Disappointment turned into anger and back again while they marked the spot and radioed for a truck to come and collect the meat. I turned down the offer for the skin and horns, wanting to get away from that place and the PH and the young kudu lying unnecessarily dead among the fallen leaves in the winter-brown grass.

We clubbed a brace of puff adders and took their skins, then connected with some of the others to have lunch and plan the afternoon. Nearby were two waterholes where kudu often came to drink in the heat of the day. It sounded promising and it was suggested that I should sit near the larger of the two. We walked in together and soon came to a fork in the faint trail.

"I've changed my mind," declared the PH without mentioning why. I was to go to the little waterhole instead. Twenty minutes later, while we were watching lizards chase each other, my friend shot "my" kudu. We heard the shot and the bullet hitting bone. It was that close.

Many have written of kudu, but it isn't much of a stretch to rank Hemingway and Ruark above the others. Both at various times discuss what marks a kudu for a real trophy, generally agreeing that 50 inches around the curl is where things begin to get interesting. Rowland Ward has maintained African trophy records for a very long time and most consider a listing in that book an African hunter's Holy Grail. Kudu just over 54 inches qualify. This bull, this wonderful bull that should have been my bull, was 56 metal-taped inches, massive even for all that and wide at the tips. We celebrated our success late into the night for the new owner appreciated every inch of those great black horns.

The final morning came with a heavy wind. Animals were scarce. We hunted hard but had not seen anything with curling horns by the time we pulled in for a late lunch. The other truck was backed up to the skinning shed. A dozen hands were taking skins from two kudu. One head measured more than 50 inches and the other bested him by half a curl. I can't remember which, because I do not want to, but one or the other had stepped from the brush while the group walked toward a canyon to shoot varmints. Varmints – deliberately – in Africa. That bull stood still while a little rifle was exchanged for a big one, again proving it's better to be lucky than good. I suggested to the varminter that given his streak he should head for the nearest town, find a bar and buy the prettiest girl inside a drink. We would pick him up at her place, or given his age, at the hospital on our way through the following morning.

We drove out with three hours of Africa remaining. The wind had come down and game was moving. We found him this time, tall and wide with white-tipped horns pointing forward and maybe even turning out like the largest bulls. I will never know for sure. He stepped behind enough of a twig to matter at the shot. We found blood and hair, and kept after him in complete desperation until dark – even brought out a tracking dog. After we left, they searched for several days and never found a trace.

Jack Atcheson, Jr. is a great friend to have, especially for a hunter with a made-up mind about chasing something or other until he catches it. I called Jack as soon as we cleared customs to cry on his shoulder. Raised in the hunt-consulting business, he is painfully honest and warrants any amount of trust. Jack understands addictions.

"I know where you need to go for big kudu," he said after hearing the story and realizing things were critical. "My brother, Keith, was just there."

Jack told me the story and the hunt was booked before the phone hit the hook.

A year later our chartered plane landed on a gravel road. We checked our rifles for zero, then climbed into the high racks on the waiting trucks and began working through herds of gemsbok and impala and eland and other animals at a place aptly named Eden. There, high in the far corner of Namibia, next to Bushmanland and below where the magical Caprivi Strip opens into the rest of the country, kudu is king.

Seventy thousand acres, give or take a few square miles, Eden is managed exclusively for wildlife. It's one of the few places with a breeding population of black rhino, at least one of which was known to enjoy a good romp at the expense of flushing hunters.

PH Jamy Traut has lived and hunted on Eden since he was in short pants, and the place is crawling with kudu. They flock to the thickets and waterholes and dry riverbeds like vultures to gut piles. Big kudu, too, and Jamy loves to hunt them.

We got along fine, Jamy and me. He has the rare knack of asking questions and then listening to the answers, accepting things as they're presented without putting forth effort to read between lines.

"The best place for big kudu," he said early, "is not necessarily the best place to see other species. If you prefer to dedicate your time to bagging an exceptional bull, I know where we will begin."

So, while my companions watched other animals parade across big open areas and around large waterholes, we focused on kudu along the edges of the property.

The first day began with promise. A big bull, at least one that looked big when Jamy saw the tips of his horns protruding like twisted periscopes above the brush, moved off as we walked toward a feeding area. We followed, agreeing that my partner would go first on everything but kudu, provided it was something special.

We found the kudu, almost a shooter, standing near two gemsbok bulls. One of the gemsbok had it all. My friend politely crawled ahead to take us away from the muzzle blast, wrapped the sling and made the shot look easy. He didn't get the shakes until Jamy pulled the gemsbok's head clear of the brush. With the nose resting on the ground, the horn tips rose even with his shirt pockets. Rowland Ward happily took my companion's check a few weeks later.

Other hunters were bringing in game every day, and I joined them after another excellent gemsbok bull came to water the second afternoon. As we set around the fire that evening a skinner shuffled into the light, said something to Jamy and presented me with a recovered bullet.

"Your gemsbok is just under forty inches," Jamy translated. "Truly exceptional. I've hunted them all my life and never taken one so good."

One morning toward the middle of the hunt, we circled back to camp to grab our forgotten lunches and to drop off an impala ram that had stepped away from his herd long enough for a clear shot. We ate in the high rack while driving to the end of the property, parked far back from a small waterhole and walked in with axes to make a ground blind. Nearing the water, the tracker dropped to his belly and peered through the brush. He stayed there a long time looking through binoculars, then motioned me to crawl around the sprawling branches of a tree growing from the dry riverbed.

As I passed, he pressed a shaking hand to my shoulder and whispered, "This your kudu. You shoot."

At least 20 kudu were gathered at the water. The big bull, the one the tracker wanted me to shoot, was not much over 60 yards out. His horns were straight from my dreams, tall enough at a glance so there was no need to give the other bulls a second look. Through the scope, the white tips of his horns pointed straight out. The clearing exploded in dust and noise at my shot, with kudu and zebra and gemsbok running hard in whatever direction they were pointed. The bull crumbled and the bolt worked itself. Another bull hurdled him as he sunfished, trying to rock back up on his feet. The rifle jumped again and he lay still.

We pulled him to a spot that would be better for pictures while someone went back to collect the truck. A little thorn tree was nearby and I sat in its sparse shade, drinking water from a canteen for suddenly it was very hot.

Up close, the patterns in the bull's coat became complex. Nearly pure-white stripes extended through his neck and shoulders out to the tips of his dorsal mane and beard. Ears became huge radar-dish affairs. Long, thin legs seemed too delicate to carry such a large animal. His horns cast two-dimensional, lightning bolt shadows across the hot, reddish-brown sand where he had lived.

I dug out the empty cartridge that had killed him and pressed it into the ground with the butt of my rifle, a hunter's tribute learned from an old friend in Montana that just then seemed as fitting in Africa for kudu as it did for honoring his Bitterroot elk and deer.

A warthog came by, heeling three bite-size versions of herself. Smelling blood, she grunted and hustled everyone back the way they had come, little ones following in step with one another, tail flags flying. They paraded back moments later, frightened by the inbound truck but still holding the same order of march.

We splashed water on the kudu's horns to make them shine and took pictures for the less fortunate souls back home, but mostly for me. Someone said there was a steel tape in the toolbox, and Jamy asked if I wanted to know. As a matter of fact I did want to know, not that it would make any difference to me or the kudu, but because other hunters would ask.

We carefully wound the tape around each curl until it became an improbable barber pole of yellow-and-black stripes held in place by a dozen black-and-white fingers to keep things honest. Jamy was holding near the bottom and I was pressing somewhere in the middle. Neither of us could see the tips when the tape went past and I didn't understand it when the driver told Jamy that both horns were more than 56 inches. He smiled big at the news, then remembered to tell me in English.

We spent the next few days hunting for a kudu bull that Jamy thought might break 60. We never caught up with him, but another hunter did a few days after we left, and Jamy was right about him wearing 5 feet of horn.

Almost exactly a year later I was back at Eden, sitting in a brushed-up ground blind at the edge of a small clearing. A little waterhole was on the far side. Because of the close quarters, I had positioned my rifle in the shooting port as soon as I sat down. Within minutes several kudu bulls were threading through the brush and a group of cows had arrived to drink. A tremendous springbok ram was there, too, watching carefully while his harem of two dozen ewes drank and played in the water.

I tried to ignore the ram and keep track of the kudu as they faded in and out of view, but he worked his way closer and finally stood on a little mound something less than 30 yards away. I couldn't help but look at him through the binoculars. At ten times magnification, every flare of his nose, flash of his eye and flip of his tail was almost startling. He soon turned back toward the water, and as he did, a gray wall moved between us.

The bull was so close that I had to raise the binoculars to bring his head into view. He took my breath away. His horns scribed deep, sweeping curls. He walked toward the water and I could see that his back legs were gray with age. Both white tips swept up and to the right, looking for all the world as if they were blowing in a strong wind.

The bull worked through the cows, chased away a couple of small bulls, then postured to warn away others standing in the brush. He stretched his neck, lowered his head and rucked up his mane down the full length of his back. I watched him through the scope, squeezing the trigger when he turned side on. The Barnes XLC took both shoulders.

I whipped the bolt and covered him while the other animals sorted themselves out and dove away through the thornbush. Moments later I heard the springbok ram snorting. Out of the corner of my eye I found him, standing at the edge of the brush and looking back into the clearing, trying to figure out what had happened to all his girlfriends. He seemed as confused as some of the liberal pundits claimed to be the day after America told President Bush we wanted him to stick around four more years. The ram was very close and worth a try.

In most old westerns, there is a scene where a poker game turns into a gunfight. Someone says something. Brows lower. The piano player stops playing and saloon girls abandon whatever lap they were warming and scamper away in a safe direction. The combatants stare at each

8

other for awhile, then leap to their feet, chairs flying as they grab for pistols. Shots are fired. I think I did something like that, jerking the Kimber rifle backward through the hole in the brush and swinging it up and over and then back into my shoulder.

The springbok hesitated for an instant, possibly surprised as the chair that had caught on my belt flew up and out of the blind. He turned to run but I was on him, and he folded at the shot.

Because of the way this all happened, Jamy didn't know about the kudu. After looking around, he figured that I had shot an animal and needed to follow up. I let him fawn over the springbok ram until the kudu caught his attention. Then he grabbed me so hard I thought we were both going into the water. Both horns went 58 inches. About the same time at the other end of Eden, two friends pulled a double on big kudu bulls as well. What a night we had around the fire.

It has been said that the true measure of a guide or PH is whether you will pay to hunt with him again. Well, at this writing I'm booked to hunt with Jamy three more times. My next trip will be the first safari for my son and daughter, the second is for really big sable and leopard. The third? Truth to tell, there is a double rifle in my safe that the folks working under the John Rigby banner just completed. Jamy will shortly have some new concessions with good numbers of elephant and buffalo. But on all three trips we will keep looking for big kudu. Sometimes it's best to learn to live with an obsession.

Originally published in the 2007 Complete Rifleman Annual.

Jocelyn Russell
© 2009

Chapter 2

Eleanor's Bulls

I never earned anything but an A-grade on a school assignment, at least until discovering girls sometime early in my teens. That streak was almost broken during sixth grade with a report written for science class. We were given the option of any animal and I picked Cape buffalo. By God, I wrote a paper, complete with the Latin name, ballistics table and a shot placement diagram for extra credit. Even had quotes – including one by Robert Ruark recounting how a wounded buffalo had chased some unfortunate up a tree and then licked the bottom of his feet bloody with a woodrasp tongue. I guess it wasn't much of a tree. Anyway, I cited the source in proper footnote form. Knowing my teacher, Mr. Jerry Wainscott, to be a fellow hunter, I turned the paper in early so he could enjoy it at his leisure.

Wainscott gave me a "C." He said I made up the quote, calling me out in front of the whole class. Accused me of being lazy. That night, jaw locked in an underbite from all the mad, I searched the house, but the magazine had probably went out with the trash.

Determined to set things right, I stood hard against Wainscott's desk the next morning and argued the injustice bitterly, and later read the paper aloud without changes. He finally told me to let it go, or my first "C" would become my first "D." Having none of it, I stormed the principal's office at recess, scheduled an appointment for the next morning, and was there waiting when Mr. Robert W. Rumsey arrived.

An imposing man, Rumsey motioned me in, closed the door and

waved to a chair standing sentinel before his equally imposing desk. While hanging his coat on a hook, he asked what was on my mind and when he turned, seemed surprised I was still standing.

"Sir, I wrote a paper on Cape buffalo and Robert Ruark does not lie," I blurted in summation.

Rumsey looked at me in silence longer than I would have liked, then pointed to the chair again. I took the hint.

"Explain," he ordered.

I did in some detail. After I finished, Rumsey thought for some time, no doubt contemplating the injustice of it all, then asked how much I knew about hunting.

"I don't know, sir, but hunting is all that I think and dream about."

Rumsey stood, walked to a closet and took out a long wooden case. He placed it on a table, opened the lid and motioned me over.

"What do you know about this rifle?" he asked with seemingly genuine curiosity. The slight softening of his tone was appreciated, and the Winchester logo on the lid gave me a place to start.

"That's a Winchester .22, probably a Model 52 but maybe a 75," I managed. "First of either one I've seen for real. It's for shooting targets, not hunting. Too heavy to carry for very long."

Rumsey pondered the response, then went back to the closet, removed a leather shooting coat and let me try it on, hauling down the straps as much as he could around my scrawny frame. He explained the purpose of the coat, then turned the conversation to bird hunting and asked about my father's dogs. After freeing me from the coat and putting the rifle away, he scribbled something on a piece of paper, folded it, and pressed it into my hand.

"Give that to your teacher, and thank you for coming in for a visit."

Mr. Wainscott was at his desk. I waited for eye contact, then handed him the note.

He popped open the fold with his thumb, read it and then read it again after giving me a stinkeye. Crumbling the paper, he pitched it in the garbage and reached for his gradebook.

"You can go now," was all he said. I went, too, because I had read the note over Wainscott's shoulder and could not keep down a smile.

It read: "Give the boy an A, Jerry. I read that Ruark article last week."

My chance to hunt buffalo – to put everything from the past in perspective – came more than 30 years later. It was a combo hunt for plains game in Zimbabwe where nothing worked out. The big herds were loitering across the river from the concession in a national park. We cut a single bull track the first morning and followed him for three days, bumping him several times without a chance for a shot. He finally crossed the river and we never found another. Still, I had managed to hunt them. Equally important, I did it right, with a John Rigby double rifle borrowed for the occasion from company owner Geoff Miller.

Hoping for another chance at buffalo, and reasoning that my children really did not need a college education to make their way in the world, I returned the .470 and ordered my own Rigby double in .500 Nitro Express, as per Miller's suggestion. It was a long year before the rifle was finished, but worth the wait. Stocked in exhibition-grade English walnut and scroll-engraved with gold accents by Lisa Tomlin, it's as close to perfection as I will ever hold.

Through express sights and off the sticks, I fired 570-grain Woodleigh softs and solids loaded by Superior Ammunition into a cluster at 50 yards that I could have covered with a tennis ball. My son, Ross, shoots it better, but irons are a little fuzzy to my eyes.

Not being one who feels the need to name things – once to the point of creating a family dustup with the suggestion that a puppy be simplistically christened "Dog" – I was surprised when the need to properly address the rifle as something more than "the double" persisted and grew to distraction.

As it always has been with ships and was with tropical storms until political correctness slithered its way into their identification process, a right and proper name for the .500 could only be feminine to account for its beauty and grace, as well as true power. Drifting back to the Wainscott affair, I pondered the times when my buffalo dream began. It was during the 1960s, so bellwethers like people, events and music rumbled through my mind. That felt right.

Maybe she would be "Jackie" for Kennedy, or "Marilyn" with no explanation necessary. Possibly "Janis" for the Wild Turkey-drinking icon of self-destruction, though I never liked her music. There was "Mary," the name Hendrix said the wind cried. Thought came around to the Beatles. Nothing defined the decade in such wild color. That felt right, too. They sang about "Rita," but that did not ring. There was "Lucy," but I don't do drugs. There was "Prudence," ruled out for being frumpy, and "Michelle," but having dated a Michelle before meeting my wife I quickly thought better of it. There was also "Loretta" and "Jude." I liked both, then remembered they were really men. Not in a gun safe of mine, even though the one where I keep the double is stationed in the closet. Then it came, so obvious and perfect: "Eleanor," after "Eleanor Rigby." Thanks, John. Thanks, Paul.

I love Africa and manage to find my way there almost every year to hunt a wonderful property in the northeast corner of Namibia called Eden. Jamy Traut is the PH in charge thereabouts. Our friendship has grown to the point I consider him family, and the success of Eden has permitted expansion of his hunting territory to include a vast concession in nearby Bushmanland as well as sporadic opportunities in and around the fabled Caprivi Strip. Eden teems with plains game, and I've taken great trophies there. I even managed to be in camp when the opportunity for a problem elephant, a cattle-killing leopard and a lion came along. Always I asked about buffalo.

Arranging a buffalo hunt in Namibia is difficult compared to most countries in southern Africa. When the country became independent, the new government was rightly concerned about making sure its people had jobs, and more importantly enough to eat.

One of the early goals was to develop cattle ranches, but there was a problem. The buffalo in some of the earmarked areas were carriers of both TB and hoof-and-mouth disease. That prevented beef exports, something that would hamstring the industry, so drastic action was taken. A fence spanning the northeast corner of the country was built, isolating the buffalo in and around the Caprivi. Buffalo south of the fence were exterminated, and a fledgling cattle industry took hold. Herds in the Caprivi were spared, as was an isolated population in Waterburg National Park.

In 1996 the government decided that an additional population of buffalo was desirable. A farm inside the vast Nyae Nyae Conservancy was purchased and surrounded with a game-proof fence. Some migrating buffalo were trapped, tested for disease and released inside.

14

The original 26 buffalo have since grown almost tenfold, and what is now called the Buffalo Quarantine Area has expanded to 34 square miles. In concert with the World Wildlife Fund, precious black rhino were brought in, joining significant volunteer populations of leopard, hyena and plains game.

Far from a park by any definition, this area is off-limits to anyone other than a few W.W.F. workers and Park Warden Dries Alberts, who has watched over the area since 1997. Dries is also a licensed PH, so it was inevitable he would cross paths with Jamy Traut.

Knowing how much I wanted to hunt buffalo, Jamy had been looking for an opportunity to take me to the Caprivi for several years, but the concession holders had little trouble keeping a waiting list of their own clients for the limited permits. There was one other possibility: the Buffalo Quarantine Area. In 1999 Dries had determined there was a surplus of old bulls that could and should be hunted, each long past breeding age and likely to soon die naturally. The meat and the trophy fees would be welcomed by people in the nearby villages.

That first hunt was successful and a total of six bulls have been taken since. Notably, these bulls were big, with an average spread of more than 42 inches. Jamy and I talked in detail about this opportunity several times, mostly because of my concerns regarding fair chase. Finally, after hearing stories from other hunters who had been there and looking at the country for myself, I decided to give it a try. That opportunity came in 2008 while hunting plains game and leopard at Eden with my family.

After Jamy drove us through the main gate, we were swept back in time to primitive Africa. Other than a few tiny roads that permitted maintenance of scattered waterholes, there was nothing but bushveldt – thick, thorny brush with occasional openings covered in grass tall enough to hide buffalo to their backline. We had arrived at mid-morning and wanted to get started, so after a fast lunch we were off to a waterhole where Dries had found some promising tracks at first light.

Eleanor swallowed two rounds, the actions of several big bolt guns were cycled, and we took up the tracks. Four very long and hot hours later, one of the trackers came on some buffalo dung, still warm to the touch. Dries whispered that the animals were up and feeding, and the slight breeze was running in our favor.

The trackers spread out, moving slowly, trying to separate the bulls from the thick brush. Not long after, the breeze twisted and we heard them running. We found some shade and waited restlessly, hoping they would not run far.

There was enough light left for one more try, and this time luck was with us. We caught the bulls feeding in a tight cluster, indistinct black masses beyond a screen of thorns. I followed Jamy and Dries, first crouching and then crawling until we closed the distance to 30 yards. Then the real work began, sorting one from another and trying to judge the horns. I made no effort to follow the whispered conversation in Afrikaans, but it was clear from the tone that several of the bulls were big. Thankfully, one of the bulls helped make the decision for us.

There was a small opening between us and the herd, wide enough to allow a shot. We watched as several moved through, then one decided it would be a good spot to bed down. He was initially facing broadside, showing the deep curl of his horns. When he finally turned, we could see his boss was solid, the hallmark of an old bull, and that his right horn hooked out 8 inches or so past the tip of his tattered ear.

Dries had told me earlier the typical bull measured about 32 inches across the ears, meaning this one was in the high 40s.

Jamy motioned me forward. Whispering, he made sure we were both looking at the same bull and that I should take him when he stood if the shot was clear.

"Soft, then solid. We must move slightly forward to clear his shoulder."

We crawled some more until things looked good, close enough that I could see a circular chip in the top of the bull's left horn.

I slowly came up to a kneel, raised the rifle, and I thought we had him until the breeze hit me in the back of the neck again.

"He's standing," Jamy hissed, but there was no shot. The bull lunged forward, put some of the other bulls between us and thundered off.

"Sorry about that," Jamy said, watching the big animals disappear.

I was anything but sorry. After waiting for such a long time, one more day would not matter.

At daylight we were already tracking a group of bulls we hoped were the ones from the evening before. The sign was hours old, so we were all

16

surprised when one of the trackers suddenly ducked down and pointed. Nine buffalo were lined out, meandering in our direction.

I followed Dries and Jamy forward, crawling again, until we found a good spot. The bulls kept coming, including one old warrior with a boss that stood above his head like a German army helmet. They got our wind at 15 yards and stampeded away in a cloud of dust.

Dries chuckled at my surprise that we did not take one. "I don't care how long it takes," he said. "I want to get that big one we stalked yesterday."

We backtracked, picked up the trail again and learned we had found the bulls by accident. The original group we'd been following had angled away in another direction.

It was late in the afternoon by the time we caught up to the bulls. Naude' Alberts, a young master guide at Eden and distant cousin to Dries, had located them after climbing high into a tree. Picking out some landmarks, we moved closer and then ducked downwind, hoping they would come to us. It almost didn't happen and probably shouldn't have by all rights. We were looking in one direction and they appeared from another.

There were three, then five and then seven. Dries and Jamy sized them up. As they had before, several moved single-file through the only shooting lane we had, until the lead bull cut our tracks and apparently caught our scent. He turned back, head up and snorting. The other bulls stopped like they'd hit a wall, changed direction, then passed back through the opening no more than 20 yards away. All we could do was watch them go.

At the very moment I decided there would be no shot, Dries said, "That's the big one. Take him."

He did not need to say it twice. I triggered the soft-point in the right barrel, pulled the rifle down out of recoil and followed with the solid from the left. The bull kicked and disappeared into the others as they bunched and ran.

Reloading quickly, this time with a pair of solids, I brought the rifle back up and covered a bull standing near the opening where I'd shot. His head was up, nose working the wind.

"That is not your buffalo, but watch him. He is looking for a fight," Dries said. We stayed put until he moved off several minutes later.

Jamy crept around Dries, his .458 at high port, and asked how I felt about the shots. I told him I felt good, but after waiting five more minutes and not hearing a death bellow, he asked again. I gave the same answer with less certainty, and just then we heard the bulls running away in the distance.

Fearing the worst, we carefully picked a path to the spot where the bull was standing at the shot. As we got close, I was more than a little surprised to see Naude', my wife, Kellie, and three trackers standing in the open.

Kellie was pumping her fist up and down in celebration, then yelled out, "That is the most incredible thing I have ever seen!"

I thought she'd gone crazy from the heat, and was certain she had no idea what a mess we were in. Five steps later I realized they were standing over my bull. Both shots had passed through his shoulders and the solid had severed his spine, driving him straight to the ground. I recognized the chip in his horn.

We all knew the bull was big, but none of us were willing to believe what we had until a square was fashioned at camp and we checked him with a steel tape. Buffalo are ranked by spread, and the Namibian national record is 48 1/2 inches. My bull's horns spanned more than 51.

The next morning we went to another waterhole, searching for an old and generally solitary bull Dries hoped to find for Ross. A bachelor band had been there so we took up the track. We eventually found the bulls, then later another bunch, but the right one was not among them. Ross took it in stride, losing himself in the hunt and savoring each approach. He joked with everyone when we stopped to take on water, assuring them this was the time of his life and there was no need to rush. He was still smiling when we drove into camp long after dark.

Dries was confident we'd find the right track the next day, so I guess we were not surprised when he did.

"It's him for sure," Dries said. "This bull is so old he drags his feet."

He might have been old but he could walk, and it took almost seven hours to catch him. We managed to get inside 30 yards without blowing him out. Ross was ready for the shot, but passed when we discovered one of the horns was broken at the bottom of the curl.

Eleanor's Bulls

We were driving to another waterhole late that afternoon when Dries spotted several bulls in the distance. One was outstanding, his horns stretching well beyond his ears. This time there was no question. Rifles were loaded and we moved to cut them off. It took most of an hour to get in front of the bulls. As we did, the big one appeared from cover broadside, much closer than we expected.

Dries whispered something to Ross and the double thundered. The bull stumbled, swapped ends and disappeared. We waited five minutes and then a couple more for good measure, listening for the death bellow. It never came, so we edged forward to pick up the track, our heads on swivels. Ross' bull had fallen on the other side of a little knob, and we walked right up on him. He lurched to his feet, but Ross was ready. He hit him with a solid and immediately followed with another, and the bull collapsed without taking another step.

I had long dreamed of hunting buffalo, but dared not dream this big. Ross' bull was a virtual twin of mine. More than 48 inches wide, he was the seventh largest ever taken in Namibia.

Even then, standing shoulder-to-shoulder with my son while we each took our first buffalo is what really made a lifetime of waiting worthwhile. 🐃

Originally published as "Fated a Dreamer" in the November/December 2008 issue of Sporting Classics.

Chapter 3

Elk Beyond Compare

If one were to imagine New Mexico as the face of a clock, Fence Lake would be a speck centering the eye of the nine. Smack on the Arizona border and just beneath the Zuni and Ramah reservations, from that tiny town you can squint against the rising sun and see the Continental Divide tracing a serpent's path across the high plains. A lonely land to be sure, more suited to antelope, wild horses and a backdrop for western pulps than anything else. The Hubble Ranch rambles eastward from Fence Lake, following Highways 37 and 117 like a stray dog. It straddles the Divide and lines out toward Albuquerque, then shows good judgment by pulling up short. Three-hundred-thousand acres of working ranch pimpled with volcanic mounds and juniper clumps, it's home to naive coyotes and real cowboys.

There is a little country store at the junction of 37 and 117 well worth a stop. While the lady who runs the place is something of a pleasant distraction, an elk set against the back wall will take your breath away. Now, I am not comparing that lady or any other with an elk. Each has its own place, merits and subjective scoring system, but this is some elk. The state record to cut it down fine – 427 gross Boone & Crockett points. It came from the Hubble just recently. Seems an archer had wrangled permission, found a ranch road and started driving. In a most improbable game of enny-meeny-miney-mo, he picked the fourth waterhole and set up a ground blind. The bull just wandered in. This story held my attention because outfitter Kirk Kelso related it while we stood in that store gazing at that elk, me with a Hubble tag buttoned down in my shirt pocket.

Born a Hunter

Kirk Kelso is an interesting man among a trade of interesting men. A full-time outfitter, he is known for running what many consider the best camps in Old Mexico for the addictive little Coues' whitetail and, for a handful of fortunate sons each year, desert bighorn sheep. His latest effort is developing a serious Kansas whitetail and bird operation, lodge and all, but he also had the good sense to lease the Hubble when it came available in 2005. He's an intense hunter, unashamed lover of fine guns and exceptionally proud of his family. Safari Club International named him their Outstanding North American Professional Hunter for 2007, a recognition that does not come easy.

One more thing sets him apart. Kelso is side-splitting, knee-slapping, tears-in-your-eyes funny. Sharing a campfire with him is like being front row center at a comedy club. He got much of it from his father, who manages the doings at camp while Kirk guides. Dad would have to be there anyway, if for no other reason than to keep the spoiled-rotten family dog out of the groceries. When the father-and-son Kelso show gets rolling, the only thing to do is sit back and latch onto something stout. Otherwise, you will soon be rolling in the dirt.

Some New Mexico ranches are known for sheer numbers of elk. Hunters there will have the opportunity to glass a bunch of bulls every day, hoping for a nice 6x6 that will look wonderful in the glow of their homefire. That is all well and good, but the Hubble is not one of those places. Nice does not cut it there. Good enough is not understood. The Hubble is a place where it might happen – not the bull of a lifetime, but of *ten* lifetimes. Putting things another way: I have dedicated much of each fall for the last 30 years to the taking a monster elk. Just one, but the real deal. I have worn through four pair of Russell boots, three trucks and a Jeep, and the patience of a long-suffering wife in the process. Public land and private, guided and self-abuse, special permit and general season, I have searched for that one great bull in almost every western state and province.

I have come close, too, but broken beams in Arizona and thin ice over a river in Alberta kept it from happening. The Hubble is, to my thinking, the finest elk hunt available today without drawing a 1-in-100 permit or throwing a brick of hundred dollar bills at an Indian reservation.

From a distance, Kelso's elk camp looks like one of the little traveling circuses that squatted in a field near the edge of town when I was a kid. Just off the blacktop, it's a loose assembly of trucks and tents and activity sprawling around a dusty cul-de-sac, a larger central tent for cooking and eating more or less in the middle of it all. Everyone came out to greet when we rolled in. Guides and dudes alike welcomed, then trundled off with a load of gear to the little white sleeping tents scattered through the junipers. It was hot, normal for New Mexico in late September.

Kelso hustled through necessary paperwork and then one of the guides led us to a proper shooting bench. Along with my partner, I was hunting with one of the new Kimber Model 8400 rifles. Mine was the six-pound stainless Montana model in .300 WSM, while his was a more traditional Classic in .300 Winchester Magnum. He went first, heating the barrel up and tweaking the Leupold scope just a bit. I fired while his rifle cooled in the shade, realizing that for only the second time in maybe a dozen years my rifle had lost zero during a flight. It took some knob-twisting, but soon the 180-grain Barnes bullets were cutting through a quarter-size hole in the target, right where they belonged.

Guns ready and able, we rounded up folding chairs, crowded into some deep shade and talked elk. Everyone had been scouting and it was plain there was competition among the guides as to where they would take their hunters to greet the rising sun of opening day. Three guides were on to big bulls, maybe really big bulls, all watched from a distance and left undisturbed the day before.

The Hubble is full of broad valleys, and from a good vantage you might search several miles in every direction. Spring and summer had been wet and green grass was still everywhere, meaning antler growth was strong but also that elk would be scattered instead of concentrated around water. The hunting was all but certain to be hard.

Everything at Kelso's camp was more than anyone had the right to expect, especially the food. They shoveled enough on our plates that first evening to bog down an army, and the gal from the store showed up to flirt with one of the guides and make the rest of us jealous. Someone at my table allowed as how it was a pity that her size was not available the day she bought her jeans. I grew tired, but listening to the show around the fire and gazing at the spectacular sky that night was worth any amount of lost sleep. We even had a front row seat for a tremendous shooting star that broke up overhead. That event was something special in the astronomy world, enough so that it was still being covered in national news a week later.

We rolled out early the next morning. The plan was to work with another hunter and guide to bracket both ends of a wide valley where two big bulls had been pushing a herd of cows a day earlier. Riding with Kirk, I was surprised to learn that we would not be calling very much. Rather, we would use our eyes and ears to locate bulls, judge them at a distance, and move quickly to head them off before they returned to thick cover. The first bugle hit when we were gearing up at the truck, and we moved on the bull as soon as light would allow. Within minutes a tan spot flickered through the juniper, and then a long, disembodied tine came into view. The bull bugled and another one we could not see said something about his momma right back. Both were within range and the wind was right, but after working in on them, we discovered neither was anything special.

By the time we made it to the vantage point, the party had already started. The others had spotted a good bull and were rock-hopping down a hillside to intercept. We found the bull quickly, and through Kirk's tripod-mounted 20x binoculars, he looked to carry nearly 60-inch main beams. Over the next hour we watched them close the distance and finally face down the bull at about 30 yards. We waited for a shot that never came, and learned later that while the bull had only five points a side, he would have scored about 350. The hunter out-loud questioned that pass for several days.

Kirk and I began the afternoon crouched in the shadow of a juniper in that same valley. We found several bulls in the distance, ruling them out one-by-one. Just as the sun was setting we discovered one that looked much bigger than the rest. Pulling on our packs, we covered the two separating miles at a fast walk, finding the group at the very last of shooting light. We had the bull cold, but he was young. Back at the truck, Kelso estimated we'd walked ten miles since hearing that first bugle – a typical day at the Hubble. My feet agreed.

The next day mirrored the first, and we searched the same valley for the pair of bulls with the big herd. Like other hunters, we saw several. While ours were not quite what we wanted, another hunter did get a long shot. The bull he missed would have made a serious run at the record book, but after carving up a big steak and thinking about it for a while, he joined us at the fire and laughed away his pain.

Changing areas the following morning, Kirk and I walked and climbed for nearly an hour. By the time the light came up, we had crowned one of the taller peaks that offered a stunning view of parks and bottoms and fields spread along northern border of the ranch. Elk were all around, but none of the bulls made the grade. A few bugled as they fed along the edges and watered, signaling the rut was ramping up to the party primary stage. We solved the world's problems, and on the way out discovered a forest full of fresh rubs and promising tracks from the night before.

We came back that afternoon full of hope and had stopped for a blow near the top when a coarse bugle tore through the trees from somewhere on the opposite slope. The wind was swirling just enough so our gunshot-wrecked ears could not pinpoint the direction. Sidehilling, we closed the distance, drawn forward by an occasional bugle.

Finally, Kelso picked out the flash of an antler in the thick pines. He threw his pack down in front of me for a rest, and I sacrificed most of the skin on my elbows and knees in an attempt to grind a shooting bench into the lava rock. I found a cow and locked in on the opening where she passed. Kirk ranged her at 437 yards, double checked, then unnecessarily hissed at me to get ready.

The elk were in no particular hurry to go anywhere, and through the scope I caught an occasional glimpse of antlers. Kirk pressed me to shoot, but the bull lagged behind the cows a long time before finally offering a clear line through one of the gaps. He humped when the Kimber jumped against my shoulder, and then disappeared behind a tree. Another round bolted, I hit him again when he stepped out, and followed two more times until he staggered and fell. Kirk called three hits and a miss.

I stayed on him for a long time to make sure he was down, knowing there would be no opportunity for additional shots once I moved. Kirk remained on the mountainside to direct traffic while I slid down to the bull. It took some time to find him, and I finally all but tripped over his antlers.

An outstanding 7x7, his sheer size was most striking. He was simply gigantic, by far the largest-bodied bull I had ever seen on the ground. Kelso said the same thing without prompting. Just 28 inches wide, the bull's 55-inch main beams and long tines later measured 355.

We hurriedly took pictures before losing the sun, and then Kirk returned to camp to get help. Hours later, he managed to lead three truckloads of hunters and guides back to help with the chores. Other than the cook, every man in camp showed up to share the moment – something of a surprise and a testament to the special camaraderie in this camp as much as hunters in general.

Feeling lucky, Kelso and I climbed the same mountain with my partner and his guide early the next morning. The rains had turned one of the bottoms into a bog, and we immediately picked up elk drinking and grazing along the edges. There were maybe 30 in the group, but the boss was nothing more than a raggy five doing his best to convince the rest of the world he was tough, much like that cheap-jacket-wearing little thug president of Iran. We all watched them for a bit, then scattered around the top to see what else we could find. Elk were everywhere in small groups that morning, but nothing was big enough to impress.

Kelso was standing behind his tall tripod when I came back, still watching the big herd by the water. Asked in a whisper if I had seen anything, my answer was halfway out when he jerked his head away from the binoculars and barked at the guide standing just below to, "Get down there and kill that elk!"

The old bull had come out of the trees on the far side of the valley and was walking stiff-legged toward the herd. Some of it was pure swagger and the rest had been earned with age. There was nothing left for him to prove. Small bulls pulled away to the edges as he parted the cows like Moses, set up in the middle and bugled. We watched as white vapor shot from his mouth, curled back through his antlers and disappeared as the first rustle of the morning breeze pushed it up and away. His belly slapped hard against the curl of his ribs to force out the final grunts as Kelso checked the others and realized they were also watching.

"Get down there!" he said. "Leave your packs and get on that bull!"

At 10x the old bull was amazing, but through Kelso's 20x binoculars he took my breath away. His main beams stretched well past 5 feet and most of his thick tines appeared to be over 20 inches long. Perfectly matched from side-to-side, we both guessed him at nearly 400 points. This was the bull I had been hunting for my whole life, and I would have paid any amount of money for another tag and the chance to scramble down the mountain after him.

It took longer than we expected for the hunters to work their way to the flat, and before we could pick out their movements, one of the little bulls ringing the near edge of the herd became nervous. He was moving back into the cows when we finally noticed the hunters creeping through the junipers to get a clear shot. The big bull trailed as the herd bunched and began to move away.

Finally a shot came, then another, then two more after the herd broke and ran. We watched the bullets kick dust just behind the bull's back feet and knew he wasn't hit.

An hour later two downcast faces told the story. Rolling ground and thick cover unapparent from our overwatch forced them into the open where they were spotted. The first shots had been long and had to be taken when the bull cleared the cows.

We found the bull again that evening, but light was fading and there was no time for a stalk. One of Kirk's hunters caught up with him the following week, and he taped out at 391 inches.

Two days later my friend redeemed himself with two spectacular shots on a fine 6x7 that went over 340, and almost every hunter in camp had a shot at a bull at least as big. Clearly, the Hubble is a place where big elk dreams can come true. After searching for a place like this most of my life, I honestly cannot wait to return. I know my giant is there, and I want to share another campfire with Kelso.

Originally published in the September/October 2007 issue of Safari *magazine.*

Jocelyn Russell
© 2009

Chapter 4

The Four Guardians of the Rosetta Stone

Ionce was imprisoned in a conversation with a man of significant importance that somehow turned to the musical brilliance of the Grateful Dead. Economic circumstance dictated positive affirmation. Endlessly, I had to agree with his observations until managing to crowbar the subject elsewhere on the fourth or fifth attempt. After the mayor of Jerrytown disappeared into the crowd, no doubt searching for other Socialists or Berkeley alumni who might be holding, a friend who had witnessed the relentless assault on both music and logic insisted on buying me dinner.

"Never," he sputtered while recalling my convincing impression of a stoned fat man playing guitar, "have I seen such masterful fakery."

Truth is, I learned long ago to ape interest and to conjure the illusion of an appropriate emotion at a hat's drop – but it was beyond me to speak a word or even muster a smile upon discovering I had drawn a desert bighorn sheep permit in Arizona after 20 years of trying. Long minutes of stunned silence were, when the dam broke, followed by hours of manic calling and messaging with news of my good fortune. While some were happy for me, most people I know are hunters, and they muttered unkind things.

There are two ways to get your name on a desert sheep tag: with a checkbook or by being lottery-drawn. Odds for the latter are long, somewhere in the hundreds or thousands against, but participation in bonus point systems can tip the odds a bit to your favor. In Arizona for instance, everyone gets one bonus point for each unsuccessful year, an extra pity point if your losing streak breaks five years, and yet another if you complete their hunter safety course. Those stubborn enough to have maximum points go into an early drawing as well, so when I found this out I flew to Arizona and took a class specially arranged for nonresidents. Years later it paid off.

Permit in hand, the first order of business is hiring the right outfitter. I called five friends with knowledge of all things related to desert sheep and received five different opinions. No surprise there, as a strong voice is an admissions requirement to *Ovis desirus extremus*, the sheep hunter's fraternity. After interviews and some sleepless nights, I sent a deposit to Chris Harlow of Double H Outfitters. We had never met so far as I could remember, but he was recommended by someone I trusted very much and what he told me about the men who would guide the hunt made the difference.

The Mattausch brothers are Dan, Dave, Bill and Ben, in order of birth. They grew up in the shadows of the sheep mountains within my permit area. As boys, their father would drive them up there on his way to work and they would spend summer days catching lizards and snakes for the local pet store, trading their bounty for candy and sodas at a nearby gas station in the finest Frank Buck fashion. As they grew older and opportunity allowed, they hunted the same mountains for deer, javelina and even sheep in the years someone was fortunate enough to draw. Their love of the outdoors pushed them down the natural path to become hunting guides, a fire that burns especially strong in Ben.

Along with members of their extended family and several close friends, one of the Mattausch clan is kicking around in the mountains flanking Tucson every day, more often than not. They started scouting the area for likely rams the weekend after I booked the hunt, more than five months before the season opened, and regularly sent reports and even photos of what they discovered.

Bighorns in this area had taken a tough hit four years ago, especially the old rams. Some 2,000 goats brought in for a ranching operation were staged in a large pen on the desert floor. The fence came down, emancipating them to the surrounding mountains.

It took helicopters and as many volunteers on the ground as could be mustered about 18 months to kill them off, as the goats quickly reverted and became as wild as the sheep. Competition for food and scarce water brought the goats in close contact with bighorns, passing diseases that proved fatal to many of the older rams weakened from their months-long rut. The brothers cautioned that finding a ram 10 years or older was going to be tough.

The crushing tide of illegal aliens appears to be having an equally troubling effect on wildlife and wildlife habitat in southern Arizona. The desert is littered with truckloads of garbage and abandoned vehicles. Illegals frequently drain the water from wildlife guzzlers for their canteens, foul the water by bathing, and in the process sometimes crack the bases, allowing the water to seep out. It is not hard to imagine that the occasional smuggler pots at a sheep or deer for camp meat, given the spooky nature of the animals we encountered. Ranchers reported that finding opened gates and cut fences are an expected part of their daily routine.

Several times the area around our camp erupted in gunfire at night. Shooting after dark is illegal, so at best it seems to be common practice for locals to break that law. For our part, we were prepared in case trouble was out there and looking for a place to happen. Things turned out well in that regard, but there is a clear need for those who value the outdoors to voice their concerns regarding this issue to their representatives.

Sheep hunting is a rifleman's game. With my permit in hand, I pondered contacting Roger Biesen in an effort to find one of his beautiful Model 70s in .270 Winchester like his father, Al, made years ago for a sheep hunter named Jack.

I also increased my efforts to purchase one of Darwin Hensley's magnificent bolt rifles. Sadly, I am still looking. Hensley is, without reservation, my favorite custom gunmaker. A life goal is to have a brace of his rifles, one for the mountains and the other for Africa.

Being practical won out. I already had a Kimber Model 8400 Montana in .300 WSM ready for an upcoming mule deer hunt in Utah, along with a few boxes of experimental loads from the Federal ballistics lab that pushed the new Barnes TSX 130-grain bullets at 3470 feet-per-second. Better still, it hit quarters at 100 yards and made change – and shot as flat as a sailcat. Topped with a Leupold VX-III 3.5-10x, it weighed just over 7 honest pounds loaded. The backup rifle would be an even lighter Kimber Model 84M Montana in .308 Winchester – that one less than 6 pounds. A second 84M would come along as well, a .22-250 Remington in case a coyote lingered.

Dave picked me up at the airport two nights before the season opened. We drove into camp an hour later, not counting a quick stop for something that did not try very hard to pass for food, and I was struck by the irony that the trophy of my lifetime might be taken within sight of a major city. Ben had a fire going against the chill and drizzle. As sheep camps go, we were in tall cotton – trailers for sleeping and tables for eating if the circle of chairs around the fire did not appeal. The whole affair was sprawled across a concrete pad covering a hole in the ground that used to hide an ICBM.

The brothers talked sheep and told stories of past hunts, often pointing off into the very dark night. Ben had taken a wonderful ram 13 years before, a prehistoric-looking beast with almost no hair, sunburned skin and record-book horns that looked like petrified wood. After kicking it up like a quail, he shot it running and momentum carried it forward into a big saguaro cactus where a horn impaled and held it upright. In a loose stack of pictures was Uncle Don's big ram from 1979, Bill's taken just last year in another area "over that way," and friend Mark Morris' spectacular sheep from the Catalina Mountains, the second largest ever arrowed. All these were mixed in with prime examples of everything else that hunting in Arizona offers today.

In addition to sheep hunting, these guys love the challenge of Coues' whitetails more than anything else. Ben recently guided two of the auction tag hunters, and Bill's buck from the previous season was sure to rank well up in the Boone & Crockett record book. Ben also had pictures and fresh video of a buck he had been watching for six years, a real monster.

It quickly became apparent that the brothers and their friends have a true appreciation for Arizona's wildlife. They spoke lovingly of the land and proudly of their efforts to conserve each species through the preservation and improvement of habitat.

Equally interesting, they also had something of their own language to describe the desert, hunting gear and characteristics of the animals. One needed the Rosetta Stone to figure it out. A prominent glassing point on the desert floor was a "bird perch," yet the same thing on the side of a mountain would be an "owl head." The outer layer of a ram's horn was "overlay" and water stations were called "tanks." Helpers without 15x binoculars who were forced to glass with spotting scopes were "one-eyed pirates." Horns were not chipped or broken or otherwise damaged. Rather, they were "chingered up." So was anything that went wrong – such as stalks that failed through no fault of our own. My favorite was the "conga line," a name hung on a stalk that included too many people.

Early the next morning someone kicked up the still-glowing ironwood fire and we ate breakfast in lantern light. Several trucks snaked up to camp, carrying brothers and uncles and friends hopelessly addicted to the sheep mountains. Nearly half had already taken their once-in-a-lifetime rams. At first light we scattered across the desert to favorite vantage points and trained tripod-mounted optics at likely spots.

I rode with Dave who followed Bill and Ben somewhere east. We found a level spot, positioned kindergarten chairs behind tripods and started taking the country apart. Homework well done, we found rams almost immediately. Two were on a nearby slope, a youngster and an old warrior with great chunks missing from his horns and what seemed to be a fresh scar cutting across the bridge of his nose. Another followed some ewes across a distant sidehill and still another fed just above the desert floor.

The last one drew our attention. He had a very dark cape and long, matched horns. Best we could tell in the coming light, his mass continued well through the quarters. More importantly, there was a big knot on a back leg, marking him as the ram that one of Dave's friends had pronounced the biggest he'd seen in many years.

Clouds darkened and soon spread a cold blanket of rain, predictably fogging the big glass. Most of the sheep moved to cover, "probably for the day," someone said, and we returned to camp and tended to the business of confirming zero. Others pulled in with tales of rams on other mountains. We tried glassing again that evening, but the rain picked up in earnest and sent us to town for dinner.

Wind and rain rocked our little trailers hard through the night. Some 3 or 4 inches came down, turning gullies into rivers, washing over paved roads and blowing out some of the faint paths we hoped to drive. For all that, everyone made it back the next morning and were ready to go, once again assembling and just as quickly disappearing into the ironwood flats. All were relieved the season was finally open.

Light revealed the ram with the chipped horn on the same mountain, as well as others scattered here and there where none had been the day before. These late arrivals were years from prime, but gave quite a show as they climbed alone or pushed ewes through the cactus patches. Rain came and went, but we wiped away at the binoculars well into the afternoon as we looked for the limping ram.

Finally, we marched toward the distant mountain, fully expecting to catch him bedded in some cuts out of the wind. Several hours of dodging puddles turned up nothing, and it was well after dark when we slogged back to the trucks. After waiting most of a lifetime for something like this, there was genuine relief that the hunt was not already over.

Dave fixed up some steaks on an old grill, enough to feed an army, really, and we tried to resolve the everlasting argument if coals were better for cooking than propane. A chorus of coyotes joined in, seeming to agree that any steak at any hunting camp was just right. Serious rain finally interrupted talk of Africa and drove us to bed.

Early the next morning we hiked back to where we left off, then continued on through a low saddle. We moved carefully, fully expecting to jump the ram with every step, the brothers figuring him for a homebody because of the bum leg. There was not much for rain, but wind pushing hard against our packs turned wet rocks into balance beams. An interesting dark spot behind some brush moved and finally turned into a free-range cow, but no rams were in sight. Ben was confident the ram was there, and he was probably right because he always seemed to be right, but there was no finding him.

One of the others had watched several rams on the back side of the

34

same mountain, so the next day we made the long drive, too, in hopes of ganging up on them and finding the one we were after. Family friend Treven Madsen glassed them up first, a long way from where we expected them to be as they glided through a saddle. One was very good from what we could see.

"Sometimes rams get happy feet," Dave said with a smile. "When they do, there is no telling how far they will go."

Between them, somehow, the brothers decided there was not a bum-legged ram in the bunch. Three days gone now, and it seemed like we were chasing a ghost.

Back at the fire, Dave and Ben decided it would be best to revisit the area where we had last seen him, split up and generally look behind every cactus until our eyeballs popped. We did just that the next day, leaving Bill and Treven down low so they could cover the entire side of the mountain in case things went bad. After climbing into the wrinkled shoulders of the main peak, we split up again. I went with Dave, but Ben found the ram. We watched the video later and agreed he was simply too young. The mass we had hoped for at the tips was not there, but what a trophy this one was destined to become. After months of scouting and four days of hunting, it was clear that the best ram was the old man we watched the first morning.

It took four more days to find the monarch again – four wonderful days of sorting through rams, calling coyotes and enjoying the beauty of the desert. More than that, one of the stalks resulted in an incredible experience.

Late one afternoon Ben made a long-distance find on a new ram, one that looked very promising. He was running with two others, and in turn they were shadowing a band of 17 ewes. We moved on them the next morning, completing a 2-hour stalk mostly in the dark. We had the wind and were in position when the light came up, maybe 400 yards from where they had bedded. The idea was to crawl over the last contour and be ready for a shot. That part seemed to work, but all the sheep came out running. I tried to get on the rams, but they rounded a bluff and stayed out of sight. The ewes stopped just short of the far horizon, looking nervously back in our direction. We were pinned for nearly three hours.

After the last one finally fed over the mountain, we picked up and started after them. Dave and I went high through the rocks, following the path taken by the rams. Ben circled just below. Somewhere along the way, I imagined hearing a thrashing in the brush. Ben caught up with us not long after, having just jumped a cougar that was feeding on his freshly killed young ram. Both of the brothers had cougar tags, one of which probably would have been used if we had made it several more steps before the cougar rushed the sheep.

Likely as not, the ram we were looking for was also in this area, provided the cougar had not spooked him, so we kept gridding the mountain from afar. It took three more days to find him, quick-stepping across a high slide several miles from where we imagined he'd gone. Even at a distance, it was easy to see the mass that carried through to the broomed tips and the difference in body size compared to the young ram trailing along behind.

Bad luck quickly fouled things up again. A thick bank of fog rolled in, hiding them from view. When it lifted we were waiting, but the mountain was empty. Leapfrogging around the base, we looked for him until dark.

Three days later, Ben and I found a ram down low. It was almost dark, and we stumbled on him more than anything else. Rain had been coming on and off that day and the sky was still heavy, so the only way to size up the ram was to stalk in and hope the swirling wind would give us a break. For my part, I thought we were looking at the biggest of the three rams buggered by the cougar. Probably by accident, we managed to get just inside shooting distance. Then the rain came, cold driving sheets that quickly soaked to the bone.

Ben had his 15x Zeiss on a tripod, looking at the ram as hard he could. I was prone in a growing puddle, hanging on his words. The reticle was settled on a shoulder, but there was no chance for me to help judge through the scope. I trusted Ben completely to make the call, a responsibility that clearly gnawed at him as he whispered dimensions between wiping his lenses and cussing the weather in general. Some minutes into this disaster, he spotted another ram bedded near the first. That one was big, too.

There was nothing to do but laugh at the irony of the moment – two great rams were right there and we could not see them clearly enough to tell which one was bigger – so I did. I laughed out loud at the rain and the wind and the hungry cougars and all the bad luck, and we snuck out of there as carefully as we could. On the way to the truck I told Ben what a wonderful time I was having and meant every word. I am not sure he believed me.

The whole bunch of us were back near the same canyon the next morning, hoping for a real look at the two rams. Separating as always, we surveyed the slopes and canyons and cliffs from far out in the desert, noticing ewes here and there, and eventually one lonely little ram. I did my impression of Karl from Sling Blade for the occasion, grumbling something about French fries and sicklehorn rams, but Dave rightfully missed both the reference and intended humor. After a while he did notice that Ben was late, so we backtracked to find him and to check in with Don and Treven. We came across Ben first, and his spotting scope was out – a good sign. It was pointed far up on the mountain, covering a ram bedded in a big saguaro patch. Since he did not say anything, I assumed the ram was nothing special.

Finally, Ben stood, tossed me his cactus cushion and said, "Take a look." After cutting down the focus, it took a while to sort the ram from the rocks, then longer still to realize he had several big chips knocked out of his horns. Ben confirmed it was the old one from the first day – the one we lost in the fog and the one I really wanted. I could not have been more surprised.

Ben found Don and Treven, repositioning them where they would watch the mountain from a distance. After council with Dave, he then took off to cover the other side in case the ram topped over during our approach. Hoping that we had seen the last of bad luck, I followed Dave up a trail that snaked pretty much in the right direction, past a tank he helped build and finally onto the slope below where the ram was bedded. We closed the distance to a half-mile and cut that in half again, using every bit of shadow and cover the mountain allowed.

At last we crawled over the ridge and I set up prone for a shot. Dave ranged a cactus near where he thought the ram was bedded at 462 yards, and we agreed there was no chance of getting closer. Rifle rested over a pack, it was easy to hold steady on a softball-size rock sticking out of the slope at about 500, even though the angle was steep. Wet from the climb, the wind soon had me shivering. Dave threw an extra shirt over my back. It did little, if anything, to help, and the wind grew stronger.

It took a long time for the ram to stand – certainly more than two hours. When he finally did, he was right where Dave thought he would be, almost aligning himself in the center of the scope. I had all the time in the world and took it, and was absolutely confident in the shot.

When Dave called it a miss I could not have been more surprised. Probably because of the wind, the ram could not tell where the shot came from. Soon he showed himself again, several steps closer. I missed again, then I missed some more. Somewhere along the way I got rattled, and I suppose it was pure accident that I nicked a leg with the fifth shot. That set him running down a canyon on our side of the mountain.

When he did not come back up the other side, Dave and I scrambled across the sidehill, me jamming more seemingly cursed rounds into the magazine and holding out hope. Hitting the crest first, Dave pointed at the ram, now standing at about 350 yards and looking at us. I went to a kneel, calmed the reticle and squeezed. The little bullet hit exactly where I was aiming, and the ram ran in a circle and fell. The only thing I could think of doing was apologizing to Dave for my poor shooting.

The ram went down in a bad place, and it took us a long time to work around the canyon and find him again. The others picked their way in from a mining access road below, and after pictures and careful field-dressing, Treven, Ben and Don took turns packing him out whole. It took several hours to come down the mountain, but everyone was in good spirits. Somewhere on the way, Treven and Don told me I was shooting into a strong crosswind – enough to whip the tops of the ironwoods behind the ram like they were in a big blender. Of course, Dave and I had not been able to see that when I was shooting, but it did make me feel a little better.

We looked the ram over the next morning, pretty much agreeing that the chips were at the quarters and probably would keep him out of the record book. We ended up being right, as he just missed, but it didn't really matter. With nearly 15-inch bases and broomed back to about 32 inches, he is the ram of my dreams. More importantly, he is a wonderful reminder of my two weeks as a member of the Mattausch clan, something even more special to my way of thinking. 🐏

Originally published as "Horn of Plenty" in the Summer 2008 issue of Under Wild Skies *magazine.*

Jocelyn Russell
© 2009

Chapter 5

Saint Vitas' Elephant

Growing up as I did in central Washington, what television stations we had came in from Spokane over a reflector. One of them ran an afternoon cartoon show hosted by a local who had commissioned himself Captain Cy. Kids lucky enough to be on the show got to walk across a bridge, meet the Captain and even introduce a cartoon if it was their birthday. With the totality of youthful enthusiasm, I wanted to experience that honor for myself, and I even remember talking about it with my buddy, Pat, while we took a break from working over the local starling population with our Crosmans. That afternoon we figured that the two greatest things in life would be meeting Captain Cy and hunting elephants. Well, Pat got to walk across that bridge and shake the Captain's hand. I managed to hunt elephants, and so I consider us even.

More truthfully, I have hunted elephants several times, hitting at it around the edges. It would have been better to dedicate a trip to the right place at the right time for the greatest of all game, but circumstance has dictated otherwise. For me, it has been a question of finding enough time while already in Africa or of finding the right elephant. Twice, bulls have fallen to others in my hunting party. Once, a big bull was located near the border of the area where I had a permit, but just on the other side. He was really something, but for whatever reason never crossed the faint two-track that would have brought him into play.

In early May, 2008, I landed at the Eden Game Ranch in Namibia in the company of three friends, each of us hoping to take some of PH Jamy Traut's fantastic plains game. Depending on how things worked out, the others were looking forward to a chance at leopards or Cape buffalo, and I had elephants on my mind. I had the right rifle for it, too: a Kimber Model 8400 Caprivi chambered in .458 Lott. Topped with a Leupold VX-7 1.5-6x locked in Talley QD mounts, it carried five rounds of Federal's great 500-grain solids in case things got country and western. For everything else I had another Caprivi in .375 H&H.

Jamy's plan was to spend several days at Eden looking for kudu, eland and gemsbok, then move some of us out to his Bushmanland concession and stare at the leopard baits. My opportunity for an elephant depended on the government declaring one of them a problem, as Jamy's single trophy permit had already been filled. It was a long shot, to be sure, and I really never gave it much thought after confirming the zero on the Lott and tucking it away in the camp vault.

Eden produced well for the others from the very first morning. A long-horned gemsbok and a warthog boar with teeth that would wrap around a Big Mac came in before lunch, and the skinners turned a zebra stallion into the makings of a rug that afternoon. A big waterbuck and another zebra highlighted the next day, and the first-time-to-Africa guy in our group played tag with 13 feet of python. Giraffe, kudu, eland and blue wildebeest would follow, and we all put the local jackal population on notice.

I dedicated the trip to kudu. The rut was peaking, so it stood to reason that one of the old bulls might make a mistake. Similar to whitetails in many respects, some of the largest kudu bulls are seen only during the rut.

This type of hunting presents an interesting challenge. Even though Eden is more than 100 square miles, game populations are so high that avoiding the species you're *not* hunting becomes a focal point. On top of that, a hunter must be willing to pass up opportunities to take other trophies. Holding out for a chance at a kudu bull that might be there while staring at 40-plus inches of gemsbok or a thundering big eland is tough. I thought I had mastered the art of passing up game, but I proved myself wrong the third morning.

We had slow-walked to a likely area and hunkered down in deep shade to watch some kudu cows. Young bulls were there, too, uncertain as boys working between gaggles of girls at a junior high dance. The bulls were nervous, concentrating more on the surrounding brush than the cows – a good sign. I followed their gaze and caught a flash in the thorns, that of morning sun hitting black horn.

Through binoculars things got confusing. A gemsbok working our way did not look right. One horn was incredibly thick, with something symmetrical wrapped around it like the stripes of a barber pole. As it passed through an opening I saw that the gemsbok was wearing what looked to be a kudu horn, and the rifle came up.

As gemsbok often do, this one ran at the shot, and the trackers followed blood for several minutes before finding the cow. Each of her horns was about 34 inches long, and a complete kudu horn with a chunk of skull cap attached was threaded down over her left side. I was really glad to have witnesses for this one, even though the horns were jammed so tightly together that we could not budge them.

The gemsbok was in fine condition, but would not have been for long as the serrated edge of the skull had cut through the skin on her jaw and set up an infection. Jamy later suggested this was probably the result of an accident rather than a fight. More than likely, he said, the gemsbok skewered the already-dead kudu while feeding or drinking, or picked up the skull while licking the bones for calcium.

I think it was Jack O'Connor who said something about big ones looking big, a theory put to the test the next morning when we found the kudu bull. There was no hesitation. Heavy to his outturned ivory tips, he fell at the shot. It was nothing more than being at the right place at the right time, and he went over 56 inches on each side. A bull like that would normally be the highlight of any hunt, but when we brought him into camp, I learned that an elephant permit had become available. Maybe this time.

Eden is a four-hour drive from the Caprivi Strip, a place where Africa's biggest game still hold sway. Comprised of national parks and very desirable hunting concessions, this thinly settled area is home to a strong population of elephants. Some of them cause problems in the scattered villages, and when that happens the government does all it can to keep the elephants away, then as a last resort issues a hunting permit to set things right.

In this case, a group of bulls was coming out of a park and raiding the *mahango* fields near the little village of Manketti. The native San people depend on their crops to an extraordinary degree, and even a small herd of elephants can ruin the work of an entire village in several nights. The bulls had actually trampled more than they ate, and kept coming back even though the men of the village were stoking fires through the night in an attempt to frighten them away. Luckily, we could base out of a camp near a hot leopard bait, so we loaded several days' worth of supplies and headed north as fast as we could.

The villagers greeted our arrival with more than a little enthusiasm. While the children simply watched, as soon as they learned our reason for being there, every adult seized the opportunity to loudly and immediately tell their extended versions of what the demonic elephants were doing to their crops. They crowded around the tracker who spoke their wonderful clicking language, gesticulating with great emotion. With no real hope that the bulls had remained in the area through the day, we did what we could to sort out the tracks, then stationed ourselves on the highest point around and glassed until dark. Nothing showed.

We kept our promise to return at first light, picked up some men to help us look for sign, and an hour later we were walking the tracks as fast as we could. We almost caught the bulls, stepping over fresh dung and at one point thought we heard them moving just ahead. Then we came to the park fence, at least what was left of it where they went through. While resting there, one of the bulls teased us by walking out into the maintenance road just inside the fence, looking around and then disappearing back into safety. We were done for the day, so the others retreated to a leopard blind until dark while I stayed in camp and thought about elephants.

We followed the tracks again the next morning, but this time we were not even close. Calling it a bust, we drove south, me heading back to Eden and the other hunter toward a leopard blind with promising activity. Cell service along the road is sporadic, and Jamy took the opportunity to check his messages wherever possible. A good thing, too, as we learned that another group of bulls was raiding nearby, and after making a few more calls discovered that we could hunt them on the same permit. It was a long shot, but the only one we had.

Saint Vitas' Elephant

That afternoon we were listening to another group of woeful villagers telling their tales, and waited again until darkness. Back in the same spot the following morning, we found that the elephants had not returned. Deciding our only hope was to cut their tracks between the nearest waterhole and some other *mahango* fields, we took the chance. No one was more surprised than I was when one of the trackers found where the bulls had crossed.

There were two bulls this time, one much larger of foot than the other. They were moving, but still miles away from the nearest safety zone. With no other roads in the area to check, we loaded up with water and followed as fast as we could through the deep sand. It was already hot and we sweated through our shirts almost immediately.

The trackers were accustomed to the heat and set a fast pace. I managed to keep up, and my spirits lifted when we came upon some fresh sign in the first hour. Soon Jamy pressed something into my hand, a partially chewed branch that was still damp.

"We are going to catch them this time," he whispered. "Are you ready?" I allowed how I was in no uncertain terms. Just minutes later we spotted the two bulls standing in an open savannah.

At 80 yards, Jamy motioned everyone down and we went forward alone. The plan was to identify the larger bull, move in close and take him with a heart shot. Jamy instructed that I should keep shooting as long as the elephant was on his feet, probably the most unnecessary words spoken this century. With one more glance, Jamy determined that the closer bull was the one we wanted.

The wind was slight, but in our favor, and we had good cover for the next 40 yards. We worked our way closer, almost from directly behind the bull, and stopped for one last conference. Jamy asked if I wanted to try a brain shot, which naturally I did, and he quickly covered shot placement again.

I was calm, much more than I thought I would be, until the bull heard something. We had closed to 30 yards by then, and his ears flared as his head rocked around in our direction. We froze, by pure chance hidden in some shade, and he did not turn far enough to pick us up. I could see the white of his eye, and from that moment on, his eye and a spot just above and behind it were the only things in my world. I was no longer calm.

Saint Vitas is one of the Holy Helpers. Believers maintain that each of the 14 holds sway over a particular disease or ailment. Vitas' specialty is helping one gain control of central nervous system disorders, and I took the opportunity to sincerely request his best efforts on my behalf. If there ever was a time to be nervous, creeping to within 20 yards of something that weighs 5 tons and picking a target 12 feet off the ground would make the cut.

"Take him," Jamy whispered, and our rifles came up in tandem.

I settled on the spot behind the eye and squeezed. The Lott jumped back into my shoulder as the bull crumbled, and I had another round chambered by the time he recovered and came back up. I hit him again in the head, still trying for the brain, just as Jamy fired his .458 Winchester Magnum into his heart.

The bull lunged forward into a tree as my third head shot crashed, then he collapsed, taking most of the tree with him. I ran forward until the line of his spine was clear and sent the last two solids in at right angles to make sure.

Taking an elephant is a humbling experience. I was fortunate to share the hunt with close friends who understood that I needed a few minutes to collect my thoughts. After I did, we marveled together at the softness of the skin, the size of the feet and the beauty of the ivory. We took the tail in celebration, then cleaned up as best we could for pictures.

I don't remember the walk back, other than one of the guys losing the tail and somehow finding it again in the tall grass. As soon as we had a radio signal, the local warden was notified that the bull was down. He immediately gathered up several truckloads of locals who collected every scrap of meat and hide. In case you're interested, elephant is good eating.

Back at Eden that night, one of the other hunters shared pictures of a very special kudu. Taken by pure happenstance while stalking zebra, it measured well over 60 inches on the long horn – the Holy Grail of African trophies. His partner had a very good day as well, taking his first eland. As they tend to do, the leopard never showed up when someone was in a blind.

I must admit to surprise at the reactions of some upon learning I killed an elephant. Many think they're endangered or even on the brink of extinction. Nothing could be further from the truth, as several

African countries are overpopulated by tens of thousands or more. No matter, an elephant is probably on the short list of great game for most hunters. If you have a chance, trust me and take up the trail. For my part, I just got off the phone with Jamy. We are going to do it again next year.

Jocelyn Russell
©2009

Chapter 6

Born a Hunter

I have followed the belly-dragging track of a grizzly into a high Arctic basin while mountains avalanched all around. Giant bulls have come to my bugle across Arizona clearings and a full-curl Yukon Stone's ram has worn my tag. None of those things or all of them put together mean as much as a day afield with my son. He is the finest hunting partner I will ever have.

Ross is a hunter by both birth and circumstance. Grandpa Everett was at his best behind a pair of pointing dogs and Grandpa Dick loved nothing more than hunting elk in November's cold. Their fathers to the man kept guns and dogs, then that trail goes cold.

I remember well the morning of my son's birth, and my telling him that he could do anything. He spent his first 21 years proving me right in general, but the hunter he has become shades even a father's grand expectations.

That he grew up in Montana was no small advantage. We moved to Missoula just after his first birthday and were out every evening in a Jeep looking for deer and elk. During hunting season he went with me, first riding in a backpack and then under his own power, holding my hand if the track was wide enough and tottering along behind if I had to break trail through the snow. He helped me pack out deer, elk and black bear, and he was there when his mother took a moose. At age 3 his eyes lit up over an old Daisy BB gun Grandpa Dick kept at his cabin. They formed a plan and Ross smuggled the rifle home. It's still in his room, hung over a pair of nails driven low in the wall.

We moved to Colorado when he was 6, a mistake it took me three years to set right. While there we spent every possible day far from town in the Pawnee National Grasslands as the mountains were too crowded. That second fall I drew an antelope permit and gained permission to hunt a promising ranch. Opening day was cold and windy, but we were out there anyway, looking for a good buck marked and bedded the night before. We found him in a big open with no chance to get close enough for a shot.

Some horses picked that time to come over for a handout, and Ross remembered without prompting a story I had told him about how Indians used horses for cover when approaching game. Gambling, we hunkered over and walked straight at the antelope, Ross holding onto my belt and nervous about the horses on his heels. It worked perfectly, and that buck still stands as the best I've taken.

When Ross was 9 we returned to Montana, putting down roots in a house crowded against the spine of the Rockies near Kalispell. Whitetail bucks frequented the yard and a grizzly came up on the deck one memorable night. Ross soon confided that returning to Montana let him remember how to dream. Then and there, I knew I had done him right. He set up an elaborate shooting range, practicing more often than not with his little sister. That fall he joined the 4-H shooting sports program and won his division in the state rifle match. He trapped skunks, fed raccoons and caught turtles in a little lake just over the hill. We revived the tradition of going out in the evening to look for game and hunted together every day when the seasons rolled around.

Kalispell proved to be a great place to raise a family. People are as good as you will find anywhere and the school system is outstanding. Things that should matter still do. Folks know how to look out for their neighbors but can keep to themselves. Rock and roll thunders over the speakers at high school football games, but if you forgot to remove your hat during the National Anthem, someone is likely to do it for you. Ross thrived. He found great friends, never got in trouble and I never once heard him call rap music.

You have to turn 12 before getting a hunting license in Montana, and waiting those last three years was pretty tough on him. The summer before he could carry his own rifle we spent quite a bit of time practicing with a good-shooting .270 that fit him well. He had his mind made up to wait for a four-point buck, and after some doing, agreed to take the first bull elk that came along. Deep into the season, I talked him into settling on a little whitetail buck. We were both pretty happy that day, and I gave him the knife he used to dress it out as an early Christmas present.

He took his first elk two years later with that same .270, a six-point. His first mule deer came at 15, from a friend's ranch on the other side of the mountains. He also started driving and gained a good measure of freedom. I think it was around that time I admitted to myself he was growing up and would soon be leaving for college. Wanting to do something meaningful to mark the occasion, I suggested to my wife that we should take Ross and his sister, Keni, to Africa when he graduated. She agreed, though it must have been a weak moment.

Early in the summer before his senior year, like always, we put in for special hunting permits. We swung for the fence, too, applying for the best trophy areas rather than those with better odds. Ross pulled both Missouri Breaks bighorn sheep and Shiras' moose permits – two out-of-the-park home runs. We were both staggered by the opportunity.

The seasons ran concurrently, but we started with sheep. Keith and Niki Atcheson agreed to help – and help does not come any better. We met them in Lewistown, learned what they had discovered during scouting trips and followed them out to camp the next morning. It rained hard during the night, turning the roads into thick gumbo that made going difficult. Even with the late start we found a group of rams the first morning, but Ross had set a lofty goal for himself and none of them measured up.

Late that afternoon he located a band of seven rams feeding through some distant trees. There was not enough day left to move on them, so we were back at the same spot the following morning. With nothing in sight we shouldered packs and dove off into some rough country where we thought they'd gone, hoping for the best. The sheep had scattered into three groups, and it took the morning to find them all. Ross pondered what to do for a long time, then we backtracked, found the one he wanted and made a tough stalk. His 40-inch ram fell in his tracks, and we finished packing him back to the truck just before dark.

The moose hunt was much harder, mostly because he was rightfully picky. Finding several moose in good country happens pretty much every day if you do things right. Finding a Shiras' bull that looks like a real moose is another story. The season spanned more than two months and Ross shot his bull the last day. He spotted it as we were stalking another bull, when he turned to check his backtrail. I taught him that when he was little. He remembered, and thanked me for the lesson while we dressed his bull in the snow.

That Christmas I wrote a note to him and placed it under the tree:

Ross,

Today is a someday.

Since the day you were born we have whispered and dreamed and laughed out loud about what your life might bring. We have talked about school, career and fatherhood, about things we would do together someday and what fun we would have doing them.

Today is one of those rare, magical days in life when a dream gets to stick around after you wake up. Today is a someday. So, pause for a moment and take it all in. It is Christmas. Your family is here and healthy. You hold the world by the tail. You really can do anything.

It is not much of a stretch to tie the words "give" and "gift" together. The intent of a gift is to give something representative of love, respect or appreciation. Our gift to you today is for all these reasons.

So Merry Christmas, happy 18th birthday and congratulations on your graduation. Come June 11th, we are catching a plane to Atlanta, then Johannesburg and finally to Windhoek, Namibia. From there we will drive to Eden, where we will hunt for your gemsbok, impala, springbok, warthog and zebra – and for himself, your kudu. The tickets are in your stocking.

With more love than we will ever be able to express,
Mom & Dad

For Ross, I suppose, it took forever for our plane to leave Kalispell. We spent the weeks before planning and packing, and the months before that practicing field-shooting. His sister was going along to hunt as well, so much of the preparation was done together. Over the Atlantic they determined who would be first up on each species and managed to stick to it the entire trip.

I had hunted several times at Eden with Jamy Traut and Kamati

Tuhadeleni, and knew what to expect, but my family was overwhelmed at both the abundance and beauty of the game. I have said it before and probably will again, taking my family to Africa was the best money I've ever spent.

Two hours into the first morning we followed Jamy to a likely spot. Glassing ahead, Kamati picked out something big. We hung back while Ross moved in with Jamy. What started off as a hunt for something changed when something better showed up, then changed again when a big kudu bull surprised everyone. We heard the shot and the impact of the bullet, and Ross forever engraved his name in the records of Rowland Ward. His sister did the same thing that afternoon.

In the following days he took an exceptional eland, along with a brace of gemsbok, an impala and a gnarly old warthog. In truth, he took everything on his list and then some, plus a good sampling of birds and meat animals so welcome at the tables of Eden's residents. I was planning a return trip before we passed back through customs.

Ross left for college a few weeks after we returned. I timed his last days home to coincide with a sheep hunt in Alaska as I did not want to be there when he drove away. I thought it would help, but spent the morning he left leaning against a rock in the Brooks Range, crying. The guide and packer with me were fathers, too, and seemed to understand. I took a black wolf either that day or the next, a lifetime goal, but even that did not temper the hurt.

After several weeks at school, Ross came home for a long weekend. He joined up with a friend for an overnight hunt up the Yaak and took his first bull elk with a bow. We hunted the deer rut every chance we had later that fall, but never found anything of interest. We dedicated the following year to a giant whitetail buck discovered during a scouting trip. It was the finest game animal I had ever seen alive, but it never passed by our stands.

Using the excuse of sister's graduation from high school, we returned to Eden in the summer of 2008, the trip headlined by dangerous game. Keni had her choice of leopard or Cape buffalo, and after months of agony, settled on leopard, leaving Ross with the buffalo. Jamy had arranged for us to take two old bulls from Namibia's Buffalo Quarantine Camp in the Nyae Nyae Conservancy near the Caprivi Strip. PH Dries Alberts was on board to direct that portion of the hunt.

We practiced together with my John Rigby .500 NE double rifle, which Ross predictably shot better than I ever will. Dries had a particular old bull in mind for Ross, but once there and hunting, we found mine first by accident. Things did not work out the first day, but luck was with me the second afternoon. Measuring over 51 inches wide, my bull became the new national record. More importantly, Ross was next to me when the bull fell, something I will remember until the last moments of my life.

We tracked the bull Dries wanted for Ross for most of the next two days, finally closing with him in the thick bushveldt cover. He was perfectly huge and we probably had him, but he was badly worn down on one side. After consulting with Jamy, Dries gave Ross the option of passing in the hope of finding another. Ross rolled the dice and came up a winner.

We returned to camp for a late lunch, and afterward were driving to a waterhole when we spotted a group of bulls in the distance. One was outstanding. We loaded up our rifles and finally caught them as they grazed, the big one crossing an opening at just over 20 yards.

As he cleared, I leaned into Ross and whispered, "Never forget this moment."

Ross hit him right and proper with a 570-grain soft, and again with two solids when he tried to rise.

Amazing beyond all reason, Ross' bull was over 48 inches wide, and now ranks as the seventh largest in Namibia's all-time records. I have no doubt Ross took my whispered words to heart.

Back in Eden, Ross took the red hartebeest he wanted so much, then doubled on gemsbok with his sister. While I was sitting leopard baits with Keni, he finished the trip helping his mom take the warthog that for some reason topped her list, and then made sure that she won their bird-shooting competition.

Ross has just graduated from college and will soon have to leave Montana so he can become a doctor. Afterward, he plans to return and raise his own family. We will continue to hunt together as often as possible, and no doubt will one day take his children along – first in a backpack and then hand-in-hand if the trail is wide enough. If there is snow we will take turns breaking trail for them at least until it is Ross' turn to break trail for me.

Keep dreaming, Ross. You really can do anything. I love you.

Jocelyn Russell
© 2009

Chapter 7

The Old Man's Dream

His father and grandfather had hunted during the golden years of the American West in the mountains near the family farm in eastern Montana. Hunting was as much a part of life then as computers and cell phones are now, yet hunting meant more than providing food. He remembered how they looked forward to their hunts each fall, how he helped pack the string of horses at the trailhead, then watched them ride away, trying not to cry on the long drive home.

Returning to get them two weeks later, the horses would be burdened with meat and racks – huge racks that were hung high on the barn walls. He could still hear their voices telling the stories deep into the night while the first real snows of winter came down outside, and after being sent to bed how he would crack his door, curl up in a blanket on the floor and listen as long as he could stay awake. He could even picture how they kept their beards until nearly Christmas, both finally giving in to the nagging they secretly seemed to enjoy. He longed to be part of it, but fate got in the way. Tough times took away the farm, and along with it his chance. Like so many others, his family had been forced to move far away to find work, and the promises made to return were eventually forgotten.

The desire to hunt those mountains again never left his dad, but they had managed to hunt together when he was old enough, kicking up a grouse or bumping an occasional whitetail in a patch of woods near their modest home. A trip back to Montana never came within his father's reach, yet the legacy of hunting remained strong somewhere inside. That legacy was all his grandfather had left behind – that and a shotgun he acquired in better times and managed to hold onto through the years. What a gun it was, a beautiful little Parker double. Careful handling kept the finish full and bright, the scrolling and checkering crisp. Engraved woodcocks on the receiver were all but alive, poised in flight. Even its leather case reflected the loving attention of a man who worked hard for his money. A local doctor had learned of the double while taking care of his mother after she got sick. After handling it, he offered the equal of several months' wages in exchange, maybe more than it was worth as the strain and worry was evident on his father's face, but it meant too much and the offer was graciously turned down.

As he grew and became a man, he thought often of the far-away look in his father's eyes when the old hunting stories were told, and saw it again when he in turn had to move away to support his own young family. Like all men do, his father was aging now. He wished he lived closer, but made the long drive to visit every chance he could because the old man's greatest joy seemed to be watching his grandchildren play and retelling tales from better years. Listening heightened his desire to again see the mountains taken from him so long ago, to finally hunt Montana. Just getting by, such a hunt was much more than he could afford.

One Christmas when they came to visit, he was startled to see how much his father had aged. The sparkle was gone from his eyes and he seemed frail and much quieter than usual. At dinner he saw the old man wipe a tear from his eye – a tear in memory, he was sure, of his mom who had died several years before.

The kids were sent to bed soon after, and while his wife helped his dad with the dishes, he sneaked out to the car for the box of presents. As he placed them under the tree, he saw something that made his heart sink. A long, poorly wrapped present was mixed with others already there, partially hidden under the branches. It could only be one thing, a gun. All he could think of was how his dad looked and acted. Now he knew, his dad was going to pass the Parker to him, no doubt believing he would never be strong enough to hunt with it again. Maybe not, he rationalized; maybe it was the .22 rifle his oldest son had wanted for so long. Grandpa did want the boy to learn to shoot, so maybe he had saved up and found a good deal at the local hardware store.

The rest of the evening was miserable. He couldn't concentrate and thought up excuses to leave the room when the old man wanted to talk about hunting. After his dad went to bed, he considered confiding to his wife what he thought was going to happen, but caught himself.

The Old Man's Dream

Unable to sleep, he finally quit trying and decided to find out for sure. Going to the hallway closet where the shotgun was kept, he discovered he was right – not only was it gone but he could see the discolored outline in the paint where the case always hung. Sorry he had looked and feeling even worse than before, he crept back to bed and stared at the ceiling until finally drifting away.

The kids woke at first light. The old man was already up and dressed, looking much better and staying right on their heels down the stairs to the tree. Tradition called for Grandpa to hand out the presents, which were opened in turn. It seemed to make things last a little longer. Even though the children were having the time of their lives, he couldn't share their joy. Time after time, his father passed over the package he dreaded opening, avoiding it, until only it remained.

When the old man finally stooped to pick it and passed it to him with great care, he had difficulty choking back the tears. As he slowly removed the paper, he thought of the things he should say – *You shouldn't, Dad.* Or . . . *You still have lots of use for this, Dad.* – but he couldn't seem to make himself say anything. He glanced up and noticed the old man staring out the window, looking at something intently, something only he could see.

It was a gun case after all, but new, different than he remembered. What rested inside caught him completely by surprise. It wasn't the Parker – but a new bolt-action .30-06. He was terribly confused, then saw the note. It said simply:

Son,

Sometimes in life a man wants to do something so bad it eats him to the bone, but he talks himself out of it for one silly reason or another. This time I did the talking for you.

Love, Dad

Clipped to the note was a contract for a ten-day Montana elk hunt from an outfitter. It was marked paid. Tears came and he cried them unashamed.

The old man was still staring out the window. He reached over, put his hand on the old man's knee and said softly, "Thanks, Dad. I love you." The old man grasped his hand, squeezed, and in a faint, far-away voice said, "Son, get one big enough for both our dreams."

Originally published in the Winter 1986/1987 issue of Bugle *magazine.*

Chapter 8

Black Against the Sun

A peculiar conversational trait of well-traveled hunters is benchmarking an animal from somewhere with another from somewhere else. "A 60-inch kudu is a 40-inch white sheep," one rumbled not long ago through the perfect amber of an African campfire. "Let him go," I hissed at a friend curled behind his rifle with elbows anchored in the hot Sonora sand. "In Montana that's the mule deer of a lifetime, but down here he won't even sit the varsity bench, let alone have a chance with a cheerleader."

Agree with the specifics or not, we would all do well to applaud any genuine effort to put things in perspective while remembering the old saw about opinions and everyone having them. In the end, the only decision that matters rests with whoever is three pounds of pressure away from bang.

More to the point, how does one compare a sable if the mood strikes? Most put him well above kudu and up there with a bongo or Lord Derby eland. Some even think of a big, black bull as the equal of two from the big five and trophy fees reflect that reality. He is most certainly a trophy from nose to tail.

A worn copy of Rowland Ward's book published during my misspent college years extends sincere invitation to any sable with a horn of 42 inches or better. That might have changed, but I will see Hell before using the Internet to research something as hallowed as those records. Some things should only be found within a fine binding that shows proper respect. Someone I trust studied on this and after the point was pushed suggested with great reluctance that a 40-inch sable is equal to 62 inches of kudu or an elephant with 60 pounds a side. The table erupted as if someone had out loud insisted that the .270 is a far better rifle than any '06 ever made. It took two rounds and the telling of a great dirty joke before things settled down. Agreement was never reached.

If you can for even a moment, forget those walnut-colored horns that sweep up and then back, ringed almost to the tips and with points sharp to the touch. The mask of a prime sable bull ranks him as one of the world's most dynamic antelope. White bars bookend the black nose bridge and are in turn flanked by wide black lines running through the eyes and down the cheeks like a Bayou redneck's lambchop sideburns. The underside of his jaw is white, like the underside of the rest of him, validating the Afrikaans name *swartwitpens*, meaning "black-white-belly." He is generally black to be sure, but black is a feeble description. Catch him in the right light and he shines like a designer prom dress some rich daddy bought for his spoiled little darling. That black makes him almost invisible in the brush where he spends his days. Instead of seeing him you look through him, even when the light is good and there is nothing within 5 miles darker than a medium brown. You also think him a shadow.

He didn't begin his life black, but in browns that grew richer with age before giving completely over to black until only the backs of the ears remained chestnut. His heavy, erect mane completes the to-the-manor-born presentation, extending across his shoulders and well down the middle of his back. An old sable bull is pure pride on the hoof.

He can hear and see and smell with the best of them, which combined with his secretive nature makes him challenging and frustrating to hunt. He also has an earned reputation as a fighter. Selous wrote of a wounded sable bull turning a pack of dogs inside out in moments. I watched a grand bull come in to a waterhole, tossing his head with old-money arrogance and parting the gemsbok and kudu and wildebeest like a hot model walking the aisle at a computer game convention. A recent issue of an African hunting magazine includes a series of pictures showing a sable bluff-charging an elephant that was, according to observers, blocking him from a waterhole. They might have the bluff down, but they have the balls to back it up.

Rival sable bulls often wage fierce – even deadly – fights. It isn't uncommon to follow vultures to a bloated bull with two puncture holes somewhere deep in his gut courtesy of a rival.

My first day of sable hunting began with a tracker reporting that he had just driven through a torn chunk of road on his way to camp. Forks were exchanged for rifles and we wore most of our breakfast coffee by the time we arrived at the spot a few minutes later. The trackers and PH sorted things out and finally got around to telling us in English that two big bulls had words and then went separate directions. As soon as it was light we hurried after them with thoughts of a double, a friend one way and me the other. Neither of us saw anything until the tracks were given up miles away in the heat.

The other group came back out on a road near their truck, my friend happening to look in the opposite direction of everyone else, then innocently asking, "What is that black thing down there?"

The bull stayed in the open long enough for everyone to appreciate, but faded away when rifles peeled from shoulders. They found him again the next day, finally crawling within 30 yards. His feet and a wonderful set of horns were in the clear, but everything else was behind a wall of brush. Then the wind turned and he slipped away.

Another friend had better luck, but with a twist. They were hunting buffalo when his PH spotted a sable that he shot after a quick stalk. It was hit well, but ran into a flat, grassy area some 300 yards square. They didn't see it come out, and after a bit checked the perimeter unsuccessfully for tracks. First on foot and then in two trucks, they scoured the tall grass for the better part of two days before literally running over the dead animal with the Rover. The cape was ruined, but the 38-inch horns hang over his fireplace.

While sable were on the menu during a recent buffalo safari in Zimbabwe, the only serious hunting I have done for them has been in Namibia. I try to hunt there at least once a year with Jamy Traut at the Eden Wildlife Trust. Jamy's hunts, from trophy quality to species selection to personal attention, are unequaled. Hunting is the primary game management tool in Eden as well as the main source of income. Trophy quality for species like kudu, gemsbok, eland and waterbuck reflects this light hunting pressure and Jamy knows well the habits of Eden's animals since he was raised on the property.

While planning a hunt for our party in 2004, Jamy volunteered that Eden would allow four sable bulls to be taken during the year and that two were still available. Eden's resident herd had grown to the point that the old bulls were fighting over cows and territory and even politics for all I know, sometimes killing one another in the process. Their skulls were stacking up at the lodge. We had added the two remaining bulls to the package before the conversation was finished.

Several months later our chartered plane from Windhoek landed on Eden's strip. Hands were clasped, then we paired up and hunted in a big circle that put us into camp at dark. That night four hunters sat around the fire, two with sable bulls in mind and the other two slated for a big waterbuck. Realizing that at least two of the other hunters could take me in a fair fight, I spoke for one of the waterbuck. Surprisingly, both guys who would be hunting sable were just as focused on one of the exceptional kudu bulls that Jamy produces with regularity.

Each morning hunt began by splitting up to search for sable tracks. We found them, of course, because Jamy knew where to look. I followed jealously along behind first one then the other designated hunter until something unexpected happened. At Eden, unexpected usually means good, like shooting a 40-inch gemsbok bull casting his shadow over the sable tracks, veering off after a cheetah or more likely one of those big kudu. After three days some ten great trophies were in the skinning shed, but no sable. Tactics were changed. It was agreed that all parties would take a sable or the remaining waterbuck if the opportunity presented and the trophy measured up. Even the lucky fellow who's nearly 30-inch waterbuck bull was already salted could shoot something black. Since it was not uncommon to blunder upon a sable by pure chance, I had high hopes, but always let the others go first on the tracks.

I didn't see a bull for the rest of the trip but I did manage a 58-inch kudu and several other great trophies including a big waterbuck. The hunt was too short, a common mistake of many African trips, and we ran out of time before firing a shot at a sable. Already booked to return a year later, we simply rolled two sable into that trip and flew away.

When we came back just 12 months later, things were different. Jamy's sable herd had grown. Young bulls were maturing and trying to establish themselves, and the big bulls were moving around more than in the past, checking their borders and getting into frequent fights. Just three of us came this time, and one of the permits already had my name on it, so there was need to be polite.

The main purpose of the trip was to shake out the Kimber Model 8400 rifle in the then-new .325 WSM cartridge. We had loaded up some of the great 220-grain Swift A-Frame bullets for a spring grizzly hunt and knew they performed well, with accuracy under 1 M.O.A. Scoped with a Leupold VX III, 3.5-10x and loaded, the rifle weighed less than 8 pounds, ideal for what could be long, hot days on a track. The most startling thing about these rifles turned out to be light recoil. They churn out nearly the same energy as a .338 Winchester Magnum, yet kick about the same as a .308 Winchester shooting a mild load with a light bullet.

Jamy already knew where we would start that first morning, along a road where two big bulls frequently bumped heads. The area was being tilled up two or three times each week as the bulls fought it out, and he was convinced it would not be long before one of them killed the other.

We didn't find their tracks that first morning, but the hunt started off strong with everyone taking at least one good animal. The next morning was different. Jamy sent a tracker to check the area before light and he came back reporting that two bulls had a disagreement and left things pretty torn up. We were well along the larger track when the sun came up and Jamy's tracker, Kamati, spotted some sable cows on the other side of a dune. We were moving carefully and owned the wind, but they were staring right at us. Black as a killer's heart, the bull we were after was with them. He was too far away for a sure shot, but distance didn't matter because the brush was so thick that a tick couldn't crawl through it. All we could do was watch as he pushed his cows over the dune and downwind, his horns arching above the brush.

As soon as he disappeared we ran to cut off the angle and keep the wind in our favor. In the next two hours we got close three times, but the shooting sticks never came up. At 80 yards we had him, only needing to crawl a few feet to gain a shooting lane. Then we bumped up two gemsbok bulls that ran through the herd, scattering them.

An hour later a kudu or eland did the same thing. That time I had his shoulder clear for an instant, but the shot was offhand and not worth the risk. The last time someone stepped on a stick. I felt it pop underfoot, but the ever-polite Jamy insistently took the blame.

"Another day," he said, passing an orange from his pack. "Grand bull, wasn't he though. We will try to find him again tomorrow. Shouldn't go all that far."

Later that day I made a fantastic shot on a kudu bull I thought to be over 60 inches. Only he was 48 inches and had just switched places with the monster we'd been watching through the brush. Jamy could not figure out a way to take the blame for that one, but fortunately, I could take a second kudu. Obsessed, I hunted that 5-footer for the next ten days and never saw him again, finally settling for a heavy bull that went about 54.

Jamy thought we would find our sable in the same general area the following morning, and we were up and ready at sunrise. Another tracker, Jonah, was along this time. His deliberate style was better suited for this type of hunting as we didn't want to push the bull hard.

It took maybe two hours to find the herd. We were moving slowly into the wind when Jonah simply stopped and melted down into the brush. Jamy and I followed unquestioningly, then crawled to his side. Something was whispered in Afrikaans.

Jamy worked his binoculars for several minutes. Finally, he turned, mouthed, "Eighty yards," and motioned for me to chamber a round. Even being careful it sounded like slamming a truck door.

Our noses to the ground, Jamy cupped his hand around my good ear and whispered, "Eighty yards. He is quartering to and knows we are here. You must stand, find him and quickly take the shot. He will see you, and there will be no time for the shooting sticks." Then he pointed to a tree under which I would find him.

I came up alone, rifle leveled at the base of the tree. Peering through a Judas window in the brush, I thought he had gone. Nothing black was there, just brush with clinging dead leaves and a glint of white that, yes, bordered a black stripe surrounding a gleaming eye and continued upward, turning into a thick, ringed horn that rose alongside another, both curling away into the lowest branches of the tree. I found the rise of a powerful shoulder just over the brush, shifted sideways to clear a path for the bullet and squeezed the trigger. The bull didn't drop. He whirled and tore away.

I called the shot good. Jonah insisted it a hit. Jamy said we should wait and passed around oranges before anyone could object. Finished, we buried the peels in the sand and went to look for blood.

First there was nothing. No blood or hair to give hope. Jonah followed the bull's tracks through the sand for a long time before pointing to a red dabble along a thorn. Soon there was another, shoulder high on a leaf. We jumped him not long after, already back with the cows. He ran hard, nothing more than a glint of black here and there. Blood dripped into his tracks that now showed a front leg swinging wide.

Jonah touched my shoulder. "Here," he whispered, indicating the hit.

We soon bumped him again. Not where we expected, I had the shot but waited for Jamy to make the call. By the time he saw the bull limping it was too late.

We took a long break and followed again, catching the herd as they crossed a distant opening.

"Take him," Jamy hissed, eyes pressed into his binoculars.

Already wrapped into the sling, I ran to the side to get Jamy away from the muzzle-blast, threw the safety and locked on the black shoulder that was finally in the clear. The bull rolled, white belly flashing in the sun. It was the shot of my life.

We approached carefully to be sure, then turned him over and found the first hole high in the shoulder, maybe 10 inches above the second. He was everything I ever wanted. Jonah went for the truck while Jamy and I checked for puff adders before breaking brush to shade him from the hot winter sun.

"How long is he?" I finally thought to ask. "I am thinking 40."

"He's probably 42," Jamy replied after measuring with his hands. We were both wrong. The tape in the truck stretched to 43. We happily hunted kudu the rest of the day, knowing it could not possibly get any better.

Days later my friend took another great sable after tracking him for seven miles, and I saw several more black bulls during the trip. Jamy plans to offer more sable each year if things go according to plan, and a combination with kudu, gemsbok and eland that promises to be one of Africa's finest plains game hunts. If any openings are left, send a deposit. It will be the best money you have ever spent.

Originally published in the March/April 2006 issue of Safari *magazine.*

Jocelyn Russell
© 2009

Chapter 9

Too-Many-Bear Creek

Boyhood dreams seem destined to fade. As the years pass, their knife-edge sharpness gets worn back by the changing interests of adolescence and then even more by becoming a man. Education, responsibility, parenting and all the attending worries chip away until what once were monolithical ambitions crumble to a dust that's swept away by the winds of life. Even so, we become their product in a way that extends beyond understanding, and hopefully hold on to a few in the off chance they may one day become a reality.

On a snowy night during the winter following what we now call the Summer of Love, at pretty much the same time he did the year before and would again the year after, Gordon Eastman came to my tiny home town to show a movie about hunting and fishing in wonderful, far-away places. Mom hurried dinner for dad and I, then we went to stand in line with other fathers and their impatient sons. The high school auditorium was soon filled with images of Eastman's adventures in a land that seemed untouched by the hand of man.

Eastman and his party killed moose, white sheep and hump-backed bear trophies. Fish larger than anything we managed from the local rivers and lakes threw themselves at their flies. The men stood at the end of a rainbow, walked on glaciers and climbed mountains that reached far above the clouds. Through a young boy's eyes, they seemed to meet danger at every turn, and always with assured purpose.

After the movie ended, my best friend and I mustered up courage and worked our way to the front of a line at Eastman's table to be near the man who, I can now suppose, was our only hero at that moment.

He shook our trembling hands just like we were men and asked if we had enjoyed the show.

We probably answered, "Yes, sir." in tandem, as it was the custom of that time.

Kindly he sat down, opened a battered photo album, searched for a page and then turned it around so we could see a picture of a hunter with a great bear. Its claws seemed to reach forever. The great head was impossibly large and its body dwarfed the man kneeling behind.

To establish myself as a fellow hunter, I managed to blurt, "Grizzly?"

"No son, that's a brown bear. They're even bigger," Eastman replied, eyes sparkling. "Maybe you can get one for yourself some day. How would that be?"

Then he moved on to the next man in line who mumbled a question about hunting moose.

After scraping fresh snow from the old Dodge truck and letting it warm, Dad and I talked bear hunting on the way home. Ever the realist, he pointed out that such a hunt was most likely expensive, suggesting that, "I shouldn't get my hopes up."

But even big dreams are free, and that night like many thereafter I dreamed of hunting those giants, standing firm to a charge so determined it frightened even my grizzled guide. Writings of Annabel, Eddy and Clark would further stoke the fires of my determination. Many years later, and with the blessing of an understanding wife, actual consideration began. Of course, this is the same wife who nodded in agreement when, during a discussion of buying a house, my complete and total contribution was little more than, "I need a place to put a big bear."

Fate is a curious animal, presenting itself at times least expected. Work takes me to sports shows, and at one of them I wondered by the Barnes Bullets booth to check in with old friend Randy Brooks. He claims to run that company between hunting trips – a fact his wife, Coni, would likely and rightly dispute – but Randy does manage to globetrot a fair amount to chase things with big horns and sharp teeth.

Offering a convenient excuse for him to break away from a meeting that looked rather uninspiring, he rushed me into his temporary office to look at pictures of his brown bear. Minutes later it was all but over. He would soon be meeting with the guide who put him in front of a bear that looked as big as a Volkswagen stuck to the axles in Kodiak mud. If all went well, he would call with dates and details, and it would finally be my turn.

Randy did call, and there was an opening the following spring. That conversation is lost, other than words and phrases such as, "Kodiak, ten-footers, too close, rough weather and lots of bears." The guide was Andy Runyan.

Thirty-five years' experience in the finest big bear country on Kodiak and an unsurpassed record of finding giant bears for his hunters set Andy apart from all other guides on the island or the peninsula. More calls confirmed his ability. The deposit was away and the waiting began – 15 long months of planning and preparing and re-reading books first explored as a boy.

Kodiak Island is a raw land. Its black sand beaches line the Pacific shore, swell into brief foothills choked with alder thickets and then rise into impossibly steep, snow-laden mountains that hold their white crowns well into the season generally thought of as summer. Air taxi pilots are fond of saying that Kodiak makes its own weather, mostly bad. Wind and rain are constant companions, as much a part of Kodiak as always carrying your rifle. Excepting the odd day when the sky is out, the most you can hope for are clouds high enough and rain light enough for glassing.

Long days and short nights give ample opportunity to exercise forgotten muscles, but for the most part it's just sitting and glassing, all the while hoping to stay somewhat warm. Eventually, from nowhere a rock or a spot in a leafless alder thicket or a battered, beached log becomes a bear. Not just a bear, but the biggest thing you've ever seen. If the bear is moving away – and most of them are for there are no fences or tall-enough mountains or deep-enough snows or any sort of obstacle to keep a bear where you want him to stay or make him go where you want him to go, because only their maddening and illogical wanderlust directs them – you just have to forget him and wait for the next one. They are everywhere and nowhere at the same time.

Often you can spot them from camp, for a good camp is deliberately set among them. It is their land and they exercise their right to eminent domain with the kind of reckless abandon and justified bravado born from thousands of years of being the biggest and baddest things that walk through the valley.

Some 3,000 brown bears, the generally accepted number according to biologists who in the same breath admit they really don't know all that much about true population densities – any more than promoters at Woodstock knew how many bleary-eyed youths got drenched and stoned and screwed in the name of peace and love and music – press their pigeon-toed tracks deep into the sand, snow and muddy tundra.

The tracks themselves are something the size of grandma's pie plate. Big as your head. Front claws reach three or four inches ahead of the pad and the first time I saw one, made just hours before and not nearly far enough from the cook tent where I slept, made me question the size of the hole in the end of my rifle barrel, not to mention Andy's habit of frying bacon each morning.

The rule of thumb in judging a bear, because they all look big and are generally not near anything that allows an approximation of size, is to measure the width of the front track and add one. A bear with an 8-inch pad will square right at 9 feet. One going 9 inches was made by a sure-enough monster, for a 10-foot Kodiak boar is the equal of an 80-pound elephant or a 60-inch kudu or a 40-inch ram. Such a bear is generally ten winters old and more likely well into his teens.

On a good day in the fall a bear like that might bottom out a Fairbanks scale somewhere around 1,400 pounds. Pads on an old boar are oval, about the size of a football gone flat with ends cut off at the stripes. The pads of sows and younger boars are more in the shape of a "J." The old boar that swam the river and tracked up the bank near camp had pads over 9 inches wide. Sleeping on the ground with two layers of nylon and some goose down between you and the rest of Kodiak requires a strong sense of purpose.

Even living in good black and grizzly bear country as I do could not prepare me for the sight of my first brown. I spotted him from camp as he lumbered over some mounds at the end of a nameless bay and through a perfectly placed sliver of sunshine. The sun was low and behind me as I studied him through the 60x Swarovski, and the light seemed to dance over his windblown, wheat-colored guard hairs.

Camp was a hundred yards down the beach. After making it back in record time and spoiling Andy's dinner preparations, we trotted over to the scope so he could pronounce judgment.

"Eight-footer, maybe. Besides, he's going the other way. They walk at least four miles an hour and you can't catch them. Anyway, the chops are ready. Better call it an evening," he said.

We knew it was going to be a tough hunt from the beginning. Andy had spent most of the last 35 years living in a remote cabin not 20 miles away and he said this was the latest spring he'd ever seen. Snow reached to the tide line and stood 10 feet deep most of the way down the mountains. Room-size rafts of ice bumped down a nearby river, then stacked like tiles in the corners of the bay where our tents were anchored.

For the first ten days it alternately snowed and rained, and the wind blew hard. At night, freight train gusts running to 70 knots tore down the mountains, worked into the tents and chilled through my yuppie-down mummy bag. The bears probably didn't care. Most were still in their winter beds, but we saw at least one every day and that kept up hopes. Some were near and others 6 or 7 miles down the coast, each looking bigger than the last.

We spent our time trying to keep out of the wind as we glassed, but to hunt bears you hunt into the wind or you're wasting time. Their eyes don't help out very much, but they more than make up for it with their ears and nose. Human scent is the one thing they usually fear.

"Positive identification," Andy called it. "You won't get near a bear that even thinks it smells you, so you don't want to contaminate the hunting area by walking around."

Most days we glassed from a high spot near camp, sharing stories and jokes. From the lookout we could see where most of the biggest Kodiak bears of the last 20 years had been taken – "Just over that hill, below that lake or at the head of that valley."

We were in the right place and Andy knew it well. Besides, Andy had spent most of his life in Alaska hunting and guiding and fishing and trapping, and there was no end to his Jack London-type stories. Between stories, there was always another joke or sound political observation. Even the daily trip into the bush took on appropriate meaning. Andy called that "Building a monument to Bill Clinton."

Fitting, I thought, *but maybe too grand a tribute.*

One morning we spotted a big chocolate bear a mile across the bay. We had the wind and took off to intercept him, if there is such a thing as intercepting a bear. Kiavak, the ever-present hundred-pound golden lab romped ahead as best he could, chasing foxes and otters and migrating sea ducks until we angled behind a big pile of logs at the tide line. Shedding packs, rain gear and coats, for the first time in seven days, we chambered rounds and waited to see if our luck would improve. It did, and the bear grew larger as it shuffled down the beach in our direction.

Positioned 20 yards from where it would pass, the dog was corded up so that, as I later learned, it wouldn't try to "retrieve" the bear after the first shot the same way it retrieved my sighting target. On Kodiak, there is almost always more than one shot.

The bear came, its great head swinging side-to-side. It walked like a teenager coming home after too many beers and finding both parents waiting up, the perfect exaggeration of sobriety that doesn't fool anyone. I took pictures, and with the lens zoomed I watched the bear roll over every kelp ball in his path without finding anything of interest. To me, it looked as big as a school bus in a fur coat, but Andy wasn't sure. Something wasn't right.

It came and passed, feet splashing through the incoming tide. Then Andy took off with lead in one hand and rifle in the other to measure the track, telling me to be ready as he vaulted over the logs and hit the sand running. I ran behind, rifle in one hand and camera at eye level, shooting pictures over his shoulder. We followed the bear at a jog, and for first time I realized how no man in hip boots could ever catch a bear going anywhere in the opposite direction on that ground.

As Andy bent to measure first one track then another where it emerged from the tide, the bear turned. Through the zoom I saw its expression change from deadpan to anger. Sounding like a compressor hose being pulled from a tire, it blew and then snorted. Its mane rucked up. Its eyes narrowed with anger. For a moment it couldn't decide what to do, then moved away down the beach.

I got wide and dropped prone, then heard Andy say, "Let it go. It's a big sow. Probably nine feet."

Kiavak whined quietly. It had looked as big to him as it did to me. Then the rain came, but we sat on a little hill anyway and got soaked and laughed and glassed for hours, watching ptarmigan cocks trying to convince hens it was mating season and the hens having none of it.

Kiavak chased some foxes. A blond 8-footer walked down the mountain nearby. Sitka blacktail deer, remnants of a mostly winter-killed herd, tried to make a living from the few patches of ground not covered by snow. We called it a day when the wind grew to where it almost pushed us over, even though we sat on the leeward side of a little volcanic mound. Andy told more jokes on the way to camp and Kiavak got bit by an otter. That made him mad. He pouted the rest of the night, pride injured to the point dinner was refused, at least according to Andy.

The next morning we spotted a sow with two not-much-smaller cubs worked along a hillside across the river digging for food. We watched intently as fog washed them in and out of view.

"Might bring in a boar," Andy managed. As always he was right, and once when the clouds lifted, there was a boar with the sow. The cubs were carefully watching momma's new friend from a safe distance.

"That's not your bear. He's right at nine foot," he said with certainty. "Rubbed too. They look like hell when they're missing all that hair."

I had to agree. Soon I saw another boar farther up the valley. He came out of the riverbottom and worked his way up the mountain until he found a patch of snow where he flopped down and went to sleep.

Surely this must be the one, I hoped, but after checking him out through the spotting scope, Andy pronounced him, "Over nine, but he won't go ten. His tracks are too close together."

I didn't want to believe him, but I did. Instead we watched him sleep for most of the afternoon. Along about dinner time the wind came up and the bear plowed upward through the snow into the next drainage. Ten days later another hunter killed a bear in that valley that will most likely be the all-time number five on Kodiak. It was also the largest brown bear recorded by the Boone & Crockett Club during that awards period. I will always wonder, because I saw a picture of the hunter with that bear and it was the same color.

Early on the morning of the 12th day the wind changed direction and calmed. The sky came out, and we worked our way 2 miles up the bay to glass the next drainage. This was different country than we'd been hunting. It looked more like the plains of Wyoming than Alaska, and led down to the very tip of the island. Most of the snow was gone and the earth had become a big sponge of mounds and rocks, alder thickets and ponds. A couple of small bears, and by then I knew enough to call them that, fed across the rolling hills.

The ptarmigan were out in force and the deer enjoyed the break from full-on winter. Fishing boats and Coast Guard cutters worked up and down the shore. Bald and golden eagles soared by as we sat and laughed and ate candy and talked about all the changes Andy had seen come to his island. A gentle breeze dried two weeks of rain from our clothes and packs.

It was a grand day to be on Kodiak, but the walk back to camp that night was pretty quiet. Only three days left, I was beginning to think this wasn't going to be my year to kill a bear. Andy had never been in this area more than seven days without success, but the weather had not been on our side.

We were both exhausted, but I remembered something Clark recounted that Bill Pinnell told one of his hunters in a similar situation. "A man would be ahead to trade just one good day of hunting for weeks of bad weather on Kodiak. That's when the bears come out."

The next morning we woke to find the weather holding. We hiked down to the beach and sat up close to where we'd been the day before. A bear soon appeared several miles out, but worked away from us. Another came down the mountain by camp. Fresh trails in the snow were visible on the mountains. Kiavak chased a fox, then was humbled when the fox chased him back to us. Humiliated before Andy again, he curled his bulk against my back and slept until I gave him some cookies.

We were finishing the last of our lunch when Andy spotted a bear digging several hundred yards away. It was either a young boar or a mature sow. With its long, flowing coat, it looked more like a tundra grizzly than a brown. It fed out of sight onto a peninsula that jutted into the ocean.

Andy took a nap and when he awoke I took my turn. I woke up about a half-hour later and began rustling through my pack for a canteen. Andy looked my way, then pointed with his chin and said, "The bear is back."

I followed his gaze to the bear and without glassing thought it was the same one we'd watched earlier. It was the same color, and since Andy had told me that the big boars are usually dark brown, I didn't look at it again. Andy watched the bear as it worked up into the rocks while I concentrated on the open stretch of beach with the spotting scope. It was low tide, and if there was going to be anything down there, it would be coming out soon.

When the bear got into the rocks, Andy was finally able to get some reference to size and realized it was not the same bear as before. It was much bigger. This news was greeted with considerable enthusiasm, but the bear was out of sight before we could get our spotting scopes pointed in his direction.

"Well, I don't know how big it is, but I'm sure it wasn't the same bear," Andy said, reaching for his pack. "Let's go over there and see if we can get a better look. It could be a boar following a sow."

It took the better part of an hour to climb the ridge, but the view alone was worth it. The open Pacific stretched in front and the incoming tide sent waves sprawling up the black sand and through rocks hundreds of feet below. We sat and glassed the 2 miles of the little peninsula.

Andy remarked that if he was out there, "We've got him surrounded."

Not seeing anything, we shouldered our packs and crept over the ridge to peer into the bed of the little creek. Andy was looking down the valley toward the surf, so I concentrated on what was immediately below and behind. We hadn't gone far until I spotted a big bear lying in an alder thicket. The wind was in our favor so I tossed my "Andy rock," something I'd learned to carry in my pocket to get his attention because he was so hard of hearing. The little rock bounced off his pack and Andy turned to look at me. I pointed out the bear and we dropped behind a small bush.

The bear was sleeping on his back like a big dog. It was more than 100 yards below and almost straight down. Andy told me to chamber a round; he did the same, and after he put Kiavak on a lead, we halved the distance. Each time the bear would raise his great head we froze until he went back to sleep.

Through binoculars we could see the slick brown nose working. No doubt a boar, the dark brown color had me convinced it was a different bear, not one we had seen earlier. There was no snow nearby where we could find its track, and judging a bear lying on its back is impossible. Andy was convinced it was an old boar, probably between 9 and 10 feet.

We watched the bear for almost an hour, waiting for it to stand. We tried everything to judge its size, including subtending its body length with the crosshairs and measuring its head the same way. It was getting late in the hunt and Andy wanted me to shoot, but I was determined to wait until there no guess about size and make sure he wasn't rubbed.

I suggested we work closer until we got him to stand but Andy insisted on waiting him out. He didn't want to shoot a startled bear, more than anything because they can be harder to stop. We actually argued about it and continued to glass the rest of the peninsula.

Soon Andy pointed out another bear, no doubt the first one we'd seen digging. Keeping track of the sleeping bear below, we watched the other one walk out on a narrow finger with sheer cliffs on both sides that dropped 40 feet into the surf. After a few minutes of nosing around, it continued to the very end of the point, then plopped down with front legs hanging over one side and back legs over the other. Then we saw yet another bear following its trail. It came toward the bear on the point with deliberate purpose, and as it closed the distance, we realized the tremendous difference in size. The new arrival was twice as big, and some 2 feet longer through the body. Surely a big male following a hot sow.

The sow couldn't hear him coming above the surf, and he had the wind. He was almost on her before she knew he was there, and we watched through spotting scopes as she came alive in a rage. There was nowhere for her to go, so she crouched low and swung haymakers at his head. Even though we couldn't hear them, her growls were evident. Ropes of saliva blew from her mouth and streamed past the suitor's head that seemed twice as big as hers. She flopped down hard, legs extending over the cliff on each side in a gesture of submission. The boar came closer, just out of her reach. She rose again and swung, roaring.

The boar took a half-hearted but intimidating swipe at the sow, and once again she pressed her belly to the ground. They faced off, growling and pawing at each other for a time, and possibly realizing the danger of their positions, stayed just far enough apart to keep a blow from landing.

Finally, the boar backed off the point, dropped down and went to sleep like a giant dog lying up in the heat of the day, but still guarding a prized bone. The sow turned to face him, back legs dangling over the edge. She was trapped. Distracted from the bear sleeping below us, I was relieved to find him still there. He apparently could not see or hear the others fighting down in the valley.

We took pictures of the bears lying together, but the distance was great and my photos showed them only as two brown mounds overlooking the dark-blue water. We looked at the boars for a long time through the spotting scopes, trying to determine which one was larger. Neither of us could think of a single reason to hurry the hunt as hours of shooting light remained.

I ribbed Andy about this being the time when he really had to show his stuff. Clearly, there were two grand bears we could stalk. Worry knotted his face as he tried to determine which one it would be.

Impossibly, as we glassed back and forth, a third boar appeared between them. He had smelled the sow as well and moved cautiously, obviously aware of the other boars. Discovering his prize guarded, he sat down to contemplate the situation, back legs sticking forward with heels dug into the ground, black pads exposed.

Concentrating on first one bear then the other through the spotting scope, Andy growled, "I know what I am going to call this damn place – 'Too-Many-Bear Creek!'"

All three boars were about the same size, but the last one to arrive was rubbed something awful so we ruled him out. Giving nature the final say between the other two, we reasoned that the boar guarding the sow had established dominance. His coat also looked spectacular, so we agreed to a stalk. I wanted to get close anyway, but wind direction and lay of the land would force us to come over a small mound very close to the bears.

First we had to move past the rubbed boar, but Andy was confident he would leave as soon as he caught our scent. The other boar, he said, might put up a fight to protect the sow. In truth, the sow was likely a greater problem in that we would be blocking her only escape. I would have to drop the boar immediately, because he was close to a cliff hanging over the ocean. If he went over, there was no way we would get him out of the surf.

Andy figured we would first see the boar at about 10 yards. I was to shoot immediately and keep shooting until he was still. Andy would watch the sow and make sure she didn't come over the top of us.

"Hunting brownies at bayonet range," he said. "There's nothing better."

We carefully worked down the side of the canyon until we drew even with the rubbed bear. As we did, he started walking in the same general direction, and we realized our paths were going to cross. Whenever he would look our way we would stop, only moving when he moved. Soon we were out of sight among steep, house-sized mounds scattered in the creekbottom. We kept watching in every direction, and finally spotted his rubbed back coming our way. We froze in some stunted alders and let him walk past at 20 yards, working his way toward the sleeping bears. It was only then I realized the great size of the animals. Kiavak strained at his cord but didn't make a sound. We gave the bear a couple of minutes to get out of the way, climbed up into the last saddle where we had planned to leave our packs and begin the final stalk.

We quietly shed our packs and coats, checked to make sure the rifles were chamber-loaded and distributed ammunition to every pocket. Andy told another joke, a really good one that I wish I could remember, then we started to climb side-by-side. We had moved only a few steps when a bear ran over the top of the hill so hard that I could see the bottoms of its back feet. It was coming straight at us.

We threw up our rifles and I waited for Andy to tell me to shoot. The bear caught movement and slid to a stop, roaring and popping its teeth at 50 feet. It hopped stiff-legged and snorted, glaring with rage and hate and surprise. Every hair on its body was standing straight up.

"Sow . . . don't shoot," Andy whispered. "We need to get her out of here so we can get up there and find the boar."

After covering us for no more than a minute, she moved away, trying to circle and get our wind. We watched until she had gone off a safe distance, then Andy told another joke – one about Clinton taking a pair of pigs aboard Air Force One that I still remember. Then we took the last few steps to the top of the little hill and ran into the big boar.

The mound we had climbed was maybe 100 feet across the top. The boar was running up the other side looking at the sow that was now standing behind us. He had gone down the other side to drive off the rubbed boar and was full of fight. He probably knew something was wrong, because he'd heard her roar and was coming hard to chase away what he must have thought was another bear.

We had climbed between them, but we had the wind and surprised him. He couldn't seem to decide just what we were, but showed no fear. The rubbed boar was just behind him so he wheeled, trying to keep track of him, the sow and us at the same time. As he spun Andy got a good look and told me to take him.

The .375 H&H slammed against me and the Barnes X bullet broke the bear's back. He tried to get up and I hit him again. Slower this time, he tried again and when he came broadside, my third round took him through both shoulders. Not sure he was down to stay, and thinking about the other bears, I reloaded quickly while Andy covered him. The sow was running full-out several hundred yards away.

Magazines charged, we walked slowly toward the giant lying on the tundra while the rubbed boar plodded indifferently up the creek just below us. It had our wind but was in no hurry and certainly wasn't afraid. We watched it move away before looking at my bear.

I tried to lift the great head and to look at his face, but I couldn't manage it and had to settle for running my fingers through the long winter coat, comparing the length of his claws to my fingers and marveling at the size of his feet.

Leaving Andy, I grabbed my rifle and went back for our packs. On the way I remembered how all this got started 30 years before. For some reason, I just couldn't stop from saying out loud, "I got him, Dad!"

Alaska Fish and Game attaches a seal to every bear taken on Kodiak. After examining the hide and taking a small tooth from the skull, they estimated his live weight at 1,200 pounds. The close-skinned hide, without the skull, weighed 105 pounds on the airport scale after being in salt for three days. Just before the plane came, we found a level spot in front of the tent and measured the hide at exactly 10 feet square. Gordon Eastman would have been proud.

I would have liked to hunt Kodiak with Andy again, but his rule was that once you've taken a bear from his area, you can't come back. I figure he's right – one Kodiak bear should be enough for any man.

Portions of this story were published in the December 2000 issue of Petersen's Hunting; *the 2002 issue of* Petersen's Hunting Annual; *and the Summer 2008 issue of* Dangerous Game Quarterly.

Jocelyn Russell
© 2009

Chapter 10

Chasing Five Feet of Bone

Light was coming up by the time we gained the lookout and dropped our packs. The lush valley spread out below was maybe 4 miles across and at least 10 wide. It was a good place. Strips of tundra and timber-lined creeks cut it in every direction. One of the countless Alaska Range rivers tumbled down the far side on its way to the Yukon, and we could hear the whisper of rapids when the wind turned into our face. Few clouds wrinkled the pink sky, unusual for mid-September, but the ground was soaked from a week of rain.

There was a sincere chill in the air and the moose rut was coming on hard. A mile away, two big bulls were quarreling over something, more than likely a cow loitering nearby in a patch of timber. We heard the *whock* of their paddles banging together, then saw one bull lurch from behind a knot of burnt trees into a big meadow. Another followed.

They fanned out, running with the enthusiasm of home-team outfielders at the top of the first, then hooked back and came together. *Whock!* Through 10x glass they looked amazingly large, and it was soon clear the lady moose was not something either was willing to die for just yet. They pushed each other around a while longer, then walked into the timber side-by-each in that march-swagger of the deer family, heads rocking to best show off their flashing white antlers that a few days earlier had been covered in velvet.

"Reminds me of my wayward youth," I said to outfitter Fred Sorenson. "Chasing girls and acting tough with friends in an effort to impress, but not really meaning anything by it. Are we going after those moose?"

Surprisingly, Fred said no. "Those bulls go maybe forty-eight or fifty inches. That makes them legal, or nearly so, but they aren't the kind of bulls you came here to hunt. I've seen a dozen bulls in a day from this lookout and we are going to sit here every day until something special wanders by or Hell turns cold enough to keep beer."

I agreed, and fished something waterproof out of my pack so I could sit down and be comfortable for the next show.

The day before we'd hitchhiked our way to Fred's base camp via a bush plane from North Pole. It was clear from the start this hunt was going to be a winner. Fred and guide Kris Sherwood met me and two other hunters at an airstrip they'd carved out of the tundra, loading gear and supplies on a four-seat tracked rig called a Bombardier. For my part I was happy to have it, even happier that it wasn't a horse.

Minutes later we pulled into a top-class wilderness camp formed up like a circle of covered wagons along a little creek running high and fast from snowmelt. Three fresh-caped moose racks leaned against the side of a tent and the meat pole hung heavy with quarters as big as a man, all wired to a cluster of empty fuel cans.

"Grizzlies," grumbled the cook when I asked about the cans. "Lunch is hot and waiting. Help yourself."

Fred shuttled one of the successful hunters out to the airstrip so the plane didn't deadhead, said his goodbyes and quickly returned. Filling a plate, he pulled up to the table. We talked about mutual friends and shared places we had lived, then got down to moose.

It was his 11th year of outfitting in this area partnered with Henry Budney, a businessman who usually spent the season in camp. Fred had taken a top ten SCI moose while hunting with Henry in a nearby valley. Since they started up, only three hunters had gone home without a moose, each missing or passing. Since a legal moose must be 50 inches wide or have four brow tines on one side, only big bulls were hunted. Grizzly could also be taken for a trophy fee, as could caribou if you were lucky enough to draw one of the limited permits. Everyone could take a crack at a wolf if you had the right tag in your pocket.

Throughout the afternoon other hunters came and went. Two of us verified zero on our Kimber Model 84M rifles in .308 Winchester. While the caliber didn't impress Fred, he did understand why we wanted to carry rifles weighing less than 6 pounds. The tiny 100-yard groups we shot prone from atop the Bombardier helped boost his confidence, and he shared our faith in Federal's 165-grain Bear Claw bullets. Later, after a handsome dinner, we sat around the campfire and told stories of past hunts while the Aurora shot fire through the night sky.

After watching the two bulls walk into the timber, more moose appeared. A cow and her gangly twins made their way across a meadow heavy with frost, leaving a trail in their wake like a carpenter's pencil run carelessly across a clean sheet of paper. Seeing her brood brought the observation that she must be one heck of a mother to get them through summer in a country filled with wolves and bears.

Small bands of caribou flashed white in the distance. Other moose worked in and out of the timber, giving us the opportunity discuss how to judge size and learn the different ways to hunt them.

Fred's technique was proven: Spend the entire day on a lookout, and when you find the moose you want, wait for it to bed and sneak up on it. If it looks as good up close as it did through the spotting scope, have at it.

That sounds simple, but less than half of these stalks are successful. Most of the time you can't see where the bulls bed. When you do, more often than not they hear a footstep or catch some scent in the swirling wind. You don't hear them leave, they're just gone when you get there. They also tend to bed in thick cover, making a clear shot tough or impossible.

Grizzlies and wolves also hunt moose and sometimes put a bull on the run while you're creeping toward it across the tundra. It happened to us at least twice. I saw the wolf that messed things up, but the boar grizzly that crushed our fresh tracks with his 8-inch pads never came out in the open.

While wolves aren't a threat to the hunter, bears are another story and it pays to be on guard. While we were there, another hunter in the next valley was moving through thick brush and crawled right up on a sow and her cubs. He lived, but she tore him up pretty good.

We made a great stalk from the lookout on the third morning. Although I lost the coin toss to shoot first, I had to follow along.

Through the 60x Swarovski spotting scope the bull's antlers looked wonderful. He was bedded near the base of a leaning tree that we could use as a marker while crossing the flats. Three of us waded a river, worked up a dry creekbed and through a patch of burned timber until we could see the tree. From there we watched every step and turn of the wind.

We were 40 yards from the tree when Fred spotted the bull lying in a deep shadow. The wind was in our face and no one moved. Then, through the binoculars I saw his head give a slight jerk and he quickly jumped to his feet, his body screened behind a group of young trees. He crashed out of sight without giving us a chance for a shot.

Our luck changed the next morning. We were on our way to the lookout early and came in above a group of moose in a small basin. As they slipped through cover, we noticed two bulls among them.

I watched the show from a hillside while Fred led the way. It seemed to take forever for Fred and the hunter to find the bulls on the flat ground, to judge them and pick out the one they wanted. As they closed to within 80 yards, the big one heard or smelled something and raised his head above the cover. Through my binoculars I saw the Bear Claw part hair on his forehead, then heard the crack of the shot. It was a wonderful bull, at least 60 inches wide and with long, sweeping tines.

The next morning found us back at the same basin, again full of moose. We spotted two sparring bulls and several cows, and as we watched, two more bulls came into the open with their cows. Moose milled in and out of the timber. Soon, eight bulls were in front of us and a second fight broke out. One of the old boys was at least 60 inches wide, with brow tines that went on forever.

Fred and I looked over the big bull for a long time. He had just about everything, but his extraordinary brow tines didn't palmate. I decided to pass, but changed my mind as he walked out of sight. We worked our way around the hill to cut him off, but he gave us the slip.

Later that morning we went back to where the big bull had disappeared. There, we saw a huge straw-colored wolf spook several moose, but he was too far away for a shot.

Back at camp, we tallied the moose seen that day. Fred's record was 18, and we beat it by at least half-a-dozen.

Two days later our luck looked like it was going to change. The sun had only been up for a short time when we caught an antler flash far below. His spread looked good and his tines looked even better. His brows seemed deeply palmed, at least four long points playing off the front on both sides. The bull was in sight off and on for about two hours, making a big circle that brought him back to our side of the valley. He bedded in some timber where we marked him and began a stalk. An hour later we found where he'd bedded, but he was gone. Back at the lookout, Kris told us the stalk looked good, but the bull spooked when we were several hundred yards away.

Fred headed up the valley to check on a spike camp, leaving us to watch for the big bull. I didn't expect to see him again, but he showed up several miles away about the time we finished lunch. Surprisingly, he was coming back in our direction. It took him a long time to cross the valley, but it gave me the chance to carefully judge his antlers.

He eventually disappeared into a thick patch of timber and never came out. I climbed farther up the mountain and searched with the spotting scope until I found him bedded. Fred hadn't returned, so Kris and I set off after him. We crossed the river in hip waders, changed back to boots and worked our way around until we were close to where we thought he was bedded, constantly checking the wind. Kris figured the bull was somewhere just in front, and he was right. He took one step and ducked, pulling me down with him.

The bull was bedded maybe 30 yards away. We slowly stood, Kris moving slightly to the side to back me up with his .416 Rigby. The bull's antlers looked big as a porch swing as he slowly turned his head to test the wind. I held high on his shoulder and started the squeeze, then saw his head whirl back when Kris popped a stick.

The bull started to stand, and I waited to shoot until he came all the way up. My shot pushed him back down and as he struggled to regain his feet, my next shot followed the first through the shoulders. He rolled over and lay still. I think Kris is still surprised how well the little rifle did the job.

The others showed up about an hour later. From the spike camp, another hunter had taken a nice bull and a stunning gray wolf. We got everything to camp long after dark, thankful we had the Bombardier for carrying the head, hide and all the meat. A moose steak dinner was waiting, and afterward the Aurora came out again.

Our last campfire was flickering light across the moose's broad antlers while we shared stories over steaming cups of coffee. Before heading for bed, I told Fred and Kris that I wanted to come back and hunt with them again. I knew the moose would be waiting, and next time that straw-colored wolf might let me get just a little closer. 🐃

Originally published in the January/February 2003 issue of Safari.

Jocelyn Russell
© 2009

Chapter 11

Jamy's Eden

After two days of cramped airplanes, lost luggage, airport food, passport flashing and a final chartered flight highlighted by violent puking into priceless Ziploc bags, everyone had good reason to be tired and sleep should have come easily.

The pilot had buzzed the strip and almost let the dust settle before landing in the middle of the perfectly named Eden, the camp staff having just raced up and down what normally served as a gravel road to frighten off herds of springbok, zebra, wildebeest and other things Africa.

Everyone shot like Jed Clampett when we checked zeroes at the waiting bench. There was even enough time for the four of us, plus an assortment of professional hunters and trackers, to crowd atop a hunting truck and go for a drive – no doubt looking like a scene from the *Grapes of Wrath* with guns.

Kudu bulls lingered on the Kalahari's red sand, their distorted shadows making a no-less-practical platform for their wonderful flaring, twisting horns than their bodies did in reality. Gemsbok herds stood their ground, then wheeled and ran like racehorses when the truck crossed some invisible security line. Dust clouds rose far away, too, betraying movement of things big and unseen.

"Eland," said PH Jamy Traut, one of few sentences he spoke for ten days that didn't include "please," "thank you" or an apology for some imagined discourtesy.

Guinea fowl skittered away nervously through the brush and giraffe looked down from wherever they happened to be standing, as disinterested as a liberal congressman during a budget-balancing session. Warthogs, impala and jackals came and went. Hornbills flew from perches, bitching loudly.

"That's an elephant's track," said Jamy, responding to a voiced suspicion. "Please excuse me for not pointing them out earlier."

There was no shortage of game to warrant sleeplessness, nor would there be a lack of food, judging from the spectacular selection of wild meats and local garden produce found waiting in the lapa for our first dinner.

Jamy did forget to mention that a member of the camp staff was placing hot-water bottles under the thick covers at the foot of our beds in our spacious tents as a final courtesy. Later, after discovering mine with a bare foot, I had beaten it enthusiastically to death with a shooting stick, suspecting it to be a puff adder. I should mention that at breakfast the next morning, after I told the tale on myself, another hunter admitted he had pretty much done the same thing.

Anyway, none of that mattered. Rhino were keeping me awake. Specifically, a conversation about rhino.

After dinner we had retired to a patio overlooking the camp waterhole, and while watching an exceptional waterbuck tend his herd, someone asked Jamy to speak about Eden. The talk turned to one of Eden's most important accomplishments: a growing population of black rhino. I then asked what one should do upon encountering a rhino, and Jamy did his best to explain rhino etiquette.

"Good question," he began. "Stand still and they will not see you. Their eyesight is very poor, as you know. Enjoy being near them and they will soon move away."

"What if they see us?"

"Good point! Please remain still and they will soon lose interest."

"What if they don't?"

"As you might well imagine, we certainly do not want that to happen. Should a charge occur, please move quickly to the side and hide behind a bush. They will not follow."

"What if they do?"

"Another very good question! Quite honestly, they never do."

"Again, what if they do?"

"You make a wonderful point, but thankfully that has never happened."

"What is the trophy fee for a rhino?"

In fairness to Jamy, it should be pointed out that a cow rhino and her

90

nearly grown calf were "kicked up" several days later. Outdoor writer Wayne van Zwoll was one of the hunters involved in this brief but stirring encounter. He is for some reason in the habit of running marathons, so his immediate response was both predictable and successful.

The other hunter, NRA's John Zent, is a more normal sort of a guy and blessed with better judgment than to regularly exercise. John claimed to have exhausted his remaining lifetime supply of energy during what was said to be a most impressive "straight shot" toward the hunting truck, thorns be damned. The rhino had, fortunately for all concerned, followed protocol and kept going in the direction they were pointed when the race began, so everyone lived to tell about it.

Sleep finally arrived, and it seemed too short a time before the camp staff had started fires to warm large tanks of water standing behind the tents. A generator was coaxed to life and lights appeared. The hunting trucks were loaded and warmed by the time we passed on our way to the *lapa* for breakfast. Help was offered at every turn and in several languages. The worst thing about hunting Eden was putting on cold sunscreen that first morning. Everything else was easy by comparison.

Our party of four seemed to have the entire northeast corner of Namibia to ourselves. Certainly, we had Eden sewn up, as they only allow one hunting party at a time. We shared a PH and changed around so everyone had a turn hunting with a different partner. The other hunters carried Kimber's new Model 8400 Classic chambered in .300 WSM. My rifle was a petite Kimber Model 84M Classic in .308 Winchester.

Our optics wore the Gold Ring, and Leupold honcho Mike Slack was all smiles riding in the other truck, this being his first trip to Africa.

The rifles were stoked with Barnes XLC bullets hand-loaded by Kimber rifle specialist Barry Vanderstouw. Weighing a bit more than 5 pounds, my .308 was turning .30-06 velocity and the 6-pound WSMs were jacked up to the primer-flattening point as well. When we shot, stuff fell down.

Before the sun rose the first morning we'd watched impala, springbok, kudu, gemsbok and elephants. One of the impala rams was really something special, but he gave us the slip after a long stalk and nobody minded. Instead, we drove and marveled out loud over the miles-across dunes cut by a dry riverbed.

The day warmed and the birds came out. Soon they were everywhere, flashing brilliantly in the golden-hour light. Several different flavors of small antelope must have known they were not on our list and let us come right up to them before diving into cover.

"That's how they earned their family name. Duiker means diver in one of our languages," Jamy offered, eyes sweeping the horizon.

"Eland just over there. Cows. None of those grand old gray and tufted bulls we're after. Water up ahead . . . a really good place for kudu. Let's walk in and see what turns up, even though it's early. Stretch those airplane legs."

Jonah, the driver, tracker, game spotter and overall hunting genius, stopped the truck and led us through the brush, favoring the wind. We pulled ourselves along for a time, disconnecting shirts, pants, hats and skin from the thorns of every other bush.

Nearing the water, Jonah bent to look under the brush, then squatted to peer through binoculars. He said something to Jamy, who raised binoculars as well. Then Jamy did a wonderful thing. Index finger pointing upward, he made a counter clockwise upward spiraling motion over his right shoulder, indicating kudu. The only other time I remember seeing body language that clear and interesting was made by girls at our college parties.

The brush was thick and we belly-crawled through sand and sticks and goathead thorns to get into shooting position without seeing the kudu or doubting he was there. We got where Jamy wanted to be, and after a better look at the bulls, for there were now two, he realized they didn't measure up. The nearby waterbuck bull did, but we weren't hunting him that day. So did one of several springbok rams, but Jamy wanted to hunt them on another part of Eden where one in particular was carrying "too much horn for his own good."

Mostly though, we didn't shoot anything else because a gemsbok bull was standing in the shadow of the only large tree thereabouts, and he was simply outstanding. This wonderful, horse-headed, black-and-white-and-tan bull was switching the odd fly and staring down another very good bull that had come in for a drink. Then he put his nose to the ground and his horns still stood far above his back.

Jamy turned and whispered something that I couldn't hear. But I did understand when he mouthed, "Forty."

Jamy's Eden

John Zent rolled into his rifle and shot the bull in the heart, the first big game animal to be taken with a Kimber 8400. He went just a bit under 39 inches and had wonderful mass. We were done with pictures when the recovery truck showed up.

"Cape?" asked Jamy.

"Hell yes!" was John's reply.

"Good choice. Now, we will go see about eland and that springbok ram suffering under all that weight."

Topping one of the dunes, it wasn't long before Jamy sorted some eland tracks from all the others and found them to his liking.

"Old bulls," he said. We peeled sweaters and for a time followed Jamy following Jonah following eland tracks, but never caught sight. They looked for eland and I looked for rhino. Jonah spotted dust rising far in the distance as the eland moved away.

"Sorry that we didn't catch them, but there are many others about," Jamy said. "Eden has close to 2,000 eland. Lunch?"

Afternoons at Eden are ideal for watching waterholes, and in the dry Namibian desert it's amazing to see how much game they collect. Ten minutes after the truck moves away a circus parade begins. Birds come first, then springbok and warthog, then waterbuck, giraffe or zebra. Finally, kudu start appearing, their numbers growing until maybe two dozen are in sight and the big bulls begin to quarrel over the cows. At last light, an indistinct shape might become a rhino, sable, eland or elephant.

Eden may well be *the* place in Africa for kudu. Big kudu. They get that way because hunters take fewer than 40 bulls each year. A culling program keeps the bull-to-cow ratio nearly equal and Jamy just loves to hunt big stuff.

Several months before we arrived, a lady hunter was tracking eland and startled a big kudu. Jamy told her to shoot it, though it's difficult to imagine Jamy telling anyone to do anything. That bull was 62 inches.

While I was there, we spent as much time as possible at one corner of the property hunting a bull that Jamy thought was its equal. Several days after we left an Italian hunter caught up with it. That one went 60, and I have had no use for Italian food since hearing the news.

One afternoon we built an improvised ground blind. The wind

93

was running the wrong direction to use the established blind so we took advantage of a fallen tree and brushed up around it. Soon game was appearing, including a gemsbok bull that looked even larger than the one taken the first morning. The shot was easy and the bull went straight down.

I stayed in the blind until dark waiting for kudu, but the big one never came. Before the recovery truck rolled up, mouth-calling brought in five jackals. Four of them had bad luck when their eyes stilled, glowing in the beam of a big SureFire flashlight.

After Jonah pointed the headlights toward the bull, Jamy stretched a measuring tape a quarter-inch away from the magic 40-inch mark.

That same afternoon our party took a great kudu, two warthogs with good teeth and two fine impala rams. The skinning shed was busy long into the night. Jamy was thrilled with our collective success, especially since it was this same afternoon Wayne and John had to outrun the rhino.

Early one morning we spotted a kudu with deep curls. He ran before Jamy could admire him through the glasses, but first impressions were good and a stalk was launched. The brush was thick, so I stayed behind to keep down the noise.

Not long after the others had moved off, I heard roaring and sounds of what seemed to be a fight. The noise came from the opposite direction everyone had gone and a big open plain was nearby, so I wanted to believe it was a cheetah making a kill. Eden had made one available to our party so I worked my way into the wind toward the sound, ready. Soon a heard of two dozen impala appeared. Two big rams followed them into the open, fighting more often than not, and making the roaring noises every time they came together. I let them come closer and then took the larger ram. Jamy never caught up with the kudu, but my 24-inch impala made his morning.

Hunting eland is one of the great challenges of the Kalahari. Distrustful of human intent as an IRS agent auditing a Libertarian, eland can see, hear and smell you before you get out of bed in the morning and decide to hunt them. Sometimes you track them for days before getting a shot. Yet occasionally, it happens easily.

For three days Jamy tracked eland with Wayne and for three days they had no chance. They stumbled over kudu and passed them up so the herd of old eland bulls they were following would not hear the shot. They frightened big gemsbok from their day beds and became acquainted with many eland cows and young bulls.

The fourth morning John elected to give it a try and killed his eland in just over an hour, showing us just how it should be done.

On the fifth morning Jamy and Wayne caught up with an eland bull that was worth all the effort. On the way back to the truck, Wayne also took two kudu bulls well into the 50s. That was some day.

Kudu do it for me, so I concentrated on them from the beginning with hopes of bringing home a real trophy. Everything else was secondary. On the way to a waterhole for an afternoon hunt I got my chance. The day was especially warm for the Namibian winter, so the animals were drinking early. We had parked some distance away and were sneaking into the blind.

Harold usually drove the recovery truck, but was along to help carry gear and to build an alternate blind if the wind wasn't right. Working toward the blind he spotted some kudu moving along a dry river channel. Gaining a small opening, a quick glass told us that one of the bulls was superb.

The shot was not far – maybe 60 yards – but the angle was poor because the bull was walking away. I fired just as he turned to move into cover and the bullet broke his back. A second shot caught the echo of the first.

Several sets of trembling black-and-white hands gripped the tape as it rounded the last curl and finaled at just over 56 inches. With mass to spare, the bull is a trophy of a lifetime.

Like all good hunts, it was over quickly. In eight days our party took 21 animals. We even borrowed time to shoot birds when the mood struck and called predators one night.

We had a wonderful time, hunted hard and never had to lift a finger around camp or in the field. Before leaving, we had booked the same dates for the following year.

Eden deserved no less.

Originally published in the November/December 2004 issue of Safari *magazine.*

Jocelyn Russell
© 2009

Chapter 12

The Launching of Huntress Keni

Fathers with daughters being what they are, it is more than likely some will take exception to my declaration that no one has ever loved his little girl more. I honestly believe this is true and present it with absolute sincerity, but understand there may be others equally certain they merit the same distinction. That is fine and this is not a contest. What it is, really, is therapy. It is also the best hunting story I have to tell, though I do take the long way around the barn to get to the telling.

Earlier this afternoon, the most important thing in my world graduated from high school. In a few weeks she will sort through the tangle of her room, pack a random sampling and head off to college. I will remain home, protecting her with a cloak of constant worry. At this college, I fear, people called professors will set about professing things I would just as soon she not hear and hope she never comes to believe. Some of their ideas might be useful, and for 30 grand a year they should be, but a whole bunch of it will be worth about as much as that stuff you scrape off your boots after a reckless walk through a cow pasture.

It's a hedged bet that what will emerge in four years is a young woman with the tools to make her own way in life, but who still remembers where she came from. Her mother and I have done the predictables to help her navigate around the rocks that threaten to ground young people, tipping the odds in her favor. For my part, I lost all sense of reason in this effort, doing shameful things like pretending to enjoy soccer, learning to text message, and conversing with love-struck boys that showed no more sense than a young buck checking a scrape line.

Here and now, I must admit to having a good feeling about Miss Keni's future. In addition to standard daddy-brag points like being smart and self-confident and beautiful, she has a somewhat unique advantage over most of the other young ladies comprising the Class of 2012. Keni is a huntress.

Keni – shortened from Kendrik to better suit – grew up charmed in a Montana home filled with guns of every description and trophies they brought to bag. Older by three years, her brother and his friends often drafted her into their constructions of makeshift rifle ranges both inside and outside, and every fall she trampled through the mountains with us as we hunted for whatever our tags and permits said we could. Still, that she feels the way she does about hunting is not without surprise. Many of her friends were similarly advantaged, but their interest never put down much of a taproot.

Keni was simply born to the hunt, and those with similar affliction are probably nodding a quiet understanding. A fleeting sympathy to those who are not, but I guess the world needs gardeners and golfers, too.

Hunting means shooting and requisite safety, so we started on that as soon as she showed interest, even before to hear her mother tell it. BB guns came first, shots taken over a set of kid-sized sticks made by Grandpa Everett and pointed in the general direction of a swinging pig silhouette target made by Grandpa Dick. When everything happened just right, the BB slapped the pig with a wonderful *ping* and her smile warmed my heart as well as everything to the far horizon. There are some who claim the iconic American sound comes from the pipes of a Harley Davidson or the crack of a wooden baseball bat. They're mistaken. It comes from a Daisy BB gun being shot by a youngster on a summer afternoon.

Keni took her first trophy with that Daisy, a water-skipper, and soon proved it to be enough gun for frogs. When brother began shooting competitively, she took an interest in his target gun, more power always being seductive. He won the state match at age 9. Not to be outdone, she was determined to do the same thing with the same rifle and did.

Her first hunting license came when she was a dozen years old, and that fall she joined brother and I as often as possible. We agreed they would take turns each day – one having the first shot on deer, the other on elk, and whoever spotted a black bear, coyote or grouse could just cut loose. We saw many deer, of course, but Keni wanted an old buck or more likely a big one, so she did not take a deer that fall or even the next two. Elk put in an appearance almost every time she stayed home, as elk tend to do.

On the occasion of Ross' high school graduation, Christmas, birthdays and everything else we could think of as an excuse, her mother and I booked an African safari for the family the summer she turned 15. Plane tickets were under the Christmas tree, leaving 6 months to prepare. In retrospect, I declare this the best money we ever spent.

Several days after Ross graduated, we found ourselves in Windhoek, the capital city of Namibia. Professional hunter and dear friend Jamy Traut met us at the airport and we drove north and east to Eden, his spectacular 70,000 private acres set aside for wildlife. It was there that Keni came into her own as a hunter.

Between them, somewhere over the Atlantic, brother and little sister had worked out a hierarchy of animals in hopes of avoiding both confusion and argument in the heat of the hunt. Chance tapped Ross, his first-morning stalk morphing from gemsbok to zebra, and from a walk to a long crawl to, amazingly, a shot on a kudu carrying enough horn to interest the good people at Rowland Ward.

Lunching afterward in the welcome shade of Jamy's *lapa*, we wrestled off the seven-hour time change and planned the afternoon. Jamy shared that he had been trying for an exceptional kudu bull for a couple of months, a bull that was easily distinguished by its light-colored cape and golden horns. Experience is a good teacher – maybe the best – and I knew better than to make a hunt for a particular animal. But we did it anyway, and you can guess the rest.

Jamy positioned all six of us, for the party now included Kamati Tuhadeleni, the superb tracker, in a likely stand. Something less than an hour later, Kamati picked out two kudu bulls moving through thick cover. Jamy helped Keni get in position for a shot and made sure her rest was solid, completely forgetting about her father who had gotten a good look at the bull through binoculars, seen the spectacular golden horns and was experiencing the first of several mini-strokes that would continue for the next quarter-hour.

For whatever reason, the bull stopped head-on in a small opening. He stood there while Cinderella fussed with the rest, shifted her rifle and finally pushed the safety forward. She squeezed, and I do not misuse the term, a very light trigger for a very long time. The bull took the bullet hard, but immediately vanished into the heavy thorn.

"Leg," Kamati said softly.

Taught to be always respectful, Keni turned away from the pros, eyes spitting lightning bolts and searching for me. I caught her glance and she mouthed, "Heart." We gave it some time, then worked our way to where the kudu had disappeared. Tracking slowly, we found him 60 yards away, shot through the heart.

The bull's massive horns measured nearly 58 inches around the curl. He was the trophy of a lifetime, maybe of ten lifetimes.

Whatever the hunt cost, the way Keni smiled as she looked up from her kudu made it all worthwhile. I wish I had a picture of that smile, but I was having trouble with my vision just then. She did not miss that either. Wrapping me in a tight hug, she whispered, "Thank you, Daddy."

That was and remains the best day of my life, not because of the kudu, but for the memory of listening to my childrens' laughter drifting from their tent late into the night.

Going in, a kudu was the most important trophy for brother and sister alike. After that, Ross predictably focused on big antelope like eland and gemsbok, while Keni had her mind set on warthog, ostrich and what she described as a gorgeous zebra. Try as we might, Jamy and I could not come to grips with just what a gorgeous zebra might look like, but she passed judgment on herd after herd with ease, beauty being in the beholding eye.

She finally found him in a big opening, and there was no doubt in her mind. A long stalk and a longer shot followed, and she dropped him in his tracks. We took our time taking pictures, mostly because Keni did not want to leave.

An old blue wildebeest bull and a terrific springbok ram came next for her, then the warthog she wanted oh so badly. Not taken with gemsbok for some reason, she offered hers to brother, then batted her eyes at Jamy until he let her take an ostrich. Satisfied thereafter, she spent the last days shooting good-eating birds along with the odd varmint, and confounding the Eden staff by chasing and catching every lizard that crossed her path.

Ross went off to college not long after we returned home, and I set about missing him something awful. Keni tried to cheer things by turning talk to how much fun it would be to hunt the mountains together come fall. True to her word, she was ready to go early opening day. I had given her several options as to where we might go and let her pick. She was thinking whitetails and decided an all-day walk up a closed road in the Swan Valley was the just right thing to do.

We were out of the truck an hour before shooting light, me thinking how much I wanted her to take a deer and wishing the warm weather would turn to that of a proper fall. The ground was dry so we moved slowly, making little sound. We managed the first vantage point as light was coming up, gave it some glassing and then followed the narrow track along a contour climbing out of the valley.

I saw the big buck first, standing uphill in a sliver of light between two Christmas trees. Keni picked him up, no doubt by following my gaze, and slipped the slung rifle off her shoulder. I stepped back slowly to whisper in her ear as much as to clear the muzzle, and told her to shoot as soon as she was locked. She took a practiced breath, stilled the rifle and once again took more time than I would have liked before firing.

The buck ran for a moment, then piled up in a tangle of downed second growth. With absolute trust, Keni asked if he was a good buck, for she had been concentrating on the shot and never raised her binoculars. I told her to go look for herself, and reveled in her reaction when she lifted his head.

In anything but a hurry, we hauled the buck uphill to a spot that would work for pictures and celebrated the special day, her eyes never leaving the deer she had waited so long to find. By way of family tradition, I pulled a knife I'd secretly carried in my pack for the last three seasons and gave it to her. It was a gift, I explained, to celebrate and commemorate the occasion of her first deer.

That field-dressing was Keni's responsibility was never a question. We laughed and talked like we were sitting at home, waiting for the sun to top the Swans. When it did, we took a host of pictures, then shifted the deer around for dressing. I was holding the leg and Keni was just beginning the cut when we heard the elk.

I must admit that the first bugle sounded like a hunter who did not know what he was doing, and the second was not much better. That it was late in the year for bugling increased my suspicion. The third bugle was closer, just down the slope, and then I heard the cows.

I mouth-called and they answered, then the bull really opened up. Coming back to earth, I told to Keni to load her rifle again, leave everything else and get ready to move. The elk were so close I could hear them snapping branches. They were moving around the mountain, and moving fast.

Caution went away in the wind and we ran down the trail, sometimes toward and sometimes away from the herd, me knowing that her only chance for a shot was riding on us beating them to a little saddle with a small patch of open ground near the top.

I played the lay of the land back in my mind, trying to remember where we would have the best vantage. Figuring time was more important than anything else, I decided to stop as soon as the saddle came into view. That would happen at a sharp corner, so we stopped just short, duck-walked forward and settled into a kneel.

Keni's shoulder was pressed solid against mine, and her rifle came up quickly and settled on the opening without asking. A cow was already there and looking back at us. I hoped the shade we were in was deep enough to keep her guessing.

The bull bugled again, thankfully somewhere behind the cow, and when she finally took a few calm steps forward, another cow came out to join her. Another followed and a dozen more came after, pushed forward by the bull.

I whispered for Keni to get ready and to shoot as soon as she had his shoulder. Then I saw his disembodied antlers moving through the trees and realized she was going to have a shot. I wanted it to happen, more than anything I'd wanted in my life.

Keni's rifle crashed as soon as the bull was clear and my scope filled with elk running in every direction. I told her to hit him again if she saw him.

With more calm than I can describe, she said, "Dad, he's down. He's right there." He was, too, the line of his side just visible.

We closed the distance with unnecessary care, disbelief coming in waves as the dark chocolate antlers separated from the cover and kept growing. I had never even heard of anything like this happening, or dreamed it could for that matter, but the proof was lying there in front of us.

"What do we do now, Daddy?" she asked. I remember not having any idea how to answer her question.

We backtracked to the deer, gathered gear and returned to the elk, figuring it best to take care of it first. Keni pulled out her new knife and went to work on the bull. Mostly through her efforts, we had it caped and quartered in three hours, then made short work of the deer. Together, we made four packs, and had everything loaded in the truck before the sun went down.

As I write this, three years have passed since the kudu and that opening day of days. For my little girl, high school is no more and college is just two months away. I will be back to hunting by myself again this fall. Before that August goodbye, there will be one last fling for the four of us, probably the final trip we'll take together before the children have families of their own. You see, there were four tickets to Africa under the Christmas tree again this year, and Jamy said he would meet us at the airport, and then something about buffalo and leopard. I wonder which one Keni will choose.

Published as "A Huntress at Heart" in the January/February 2009 issue of Sporting Classics.

Jocelyn Russell
© 2009

Chapter 13

With Thanks to Ernesto, Jack & Mrs. Shirley Evans

Mrs. Shirley Evans was a tiny woman. The final moments of the 1960s found her working full time and raising a child alone before liberation and daytime TV made that sort of thing fashionable.

I can't remember if she had a girl or a boy, but I do know that something was always making her mad, at least it seemed like that to us boys in her fourth grade class at Lake Chelan Grade School.

Truth be told, making Mrs. Evans mad was something of a guilty pleasure. It was high sport for a 10-year-old boy to be on the receiving end of one of her chewings because most of us towered over her, or at least we did until she latched onto an ear to encourage a hasty trip to the principal's office.

One Friday afternoon something really bad must have happened. I don't recall being involved in whatever it was that lit her fuse, but Mrs. Shirley Evans turned fireplug red and marched our class three blocks to the public library. Right there on the sidewalk amongst every official building our little town had ever raised, no doubt to reinforce the gravity of the punishment, she directed everyone inside to check out a book of substantial thickness. Come Monday morning we were each to read to the class a report on at least the first 100 pages of said book. Otherwise, Hell would come collecting.

I joined the chorus of groans to keep up appearances, but I was no stranger thereabouts. Long ago I had read to tatters my father's stacks of *Sports Afield* and *Outdoor Life* magazines. The school's library was already picked through, but I had recently discovered a pretty good selection of hunting and gun books spanning a couple of shelves near the back of the building we were shortly to enter.

I hit the double doors with purpose, separated from the mob and grabbed the first book in the section that looked interesting. It was the biggest of the lot, covered with a green fake leather that was after a fashion made to look like snakeskin. The spine read *Game in the Desert*, but I couldn't have cared less about the title. Jack O'Connor's name was on it, and that was all I needed to know. Surely this book selection would impress Mrs. Shirley Evans through physical presence alone, even though I had not been the cause of all this trouble that honestly wasn't my fault.

I checked it out and knocked off at least ten pages, after looking at all the pictures of course, before the last of the condemned emerged with Nancy Drew Goes Shopping or The Hardy Boys Drill a Peephole or some other hallmark of American literature. I read more on the bus ride home, wondering what it would be like to be Brad or Jerry O'Connor – the sons who often tagged along in Jack's stories. The book was finished before Sunday dinner.

Monday morning I volunteered to go first. I wanted to show everybody how it was done, even though the trouble we were all in was none of my doing. Ignoring me, Mrs. Shirley Evans asked for a show of hands announcing who had completed the assignment. Three hands went up, mine and two of the more bookish girls. The little teacher then held forth about punishing only the guilty, messages being received, fairness and taking responsibility for our actions. With this message delivered to her apparent satisfaction, she told everyone to forget about the book report and to open our science books.

Until that book it seemed good hunts started by heading north. Canada was that direction. Beyond that, Alaska. What kind of game would live in the desert anyway? According to O'Connor, a special version of bighorn sheep and some really big mule deer. So Sonora, Mexico, was added to my "maybe someday" list.

Years later I ran across another Derrydale copy of *Game in the Desert,*

A great bull from the foothills of the Alaska Range. We watched him work through a miles-wide valley from first light until he bedded in the middle of the day, then a two-hour stalk brought us within 30 yards. Hunting moose during their rut is exciting, and Alaska is at her very best in late September.

The peaks north of Yellowstone are a stronghold for mountain goats. This old billy, taken with a Freedom Arms .454 Casull, tied the handgun world record. • Gerald Fluerty and I found this exceptional sika deer after a long day in the mountains of New Zealand. I took both red and fallow deer as well, and return to hunt with Gerald at every opportunity.

H unting desert mule deer in Sonora doesn't always end successfully, but the results can be spectacular. There is no better place to spend time in January. • This bull was raiding crops south of Namibia's Caprivi Strip, and we found him almost by chance. Having the opportunity to hunt an elephant took half a lifetime, but was unquestionably worth the wait.

An honest 10-foot-square brown bear from Kodiak Island, taken after two weeks of hard hunting in terrible weather. When the sun finally came out, so did the bears, and we had to work past two other big boars and the sow they were all chasing to get a shot. When it came, it was fast and close, just as I'd always hoped it would be.

This gemsbok cow somehow managed to get a kudu horn with a portion of the skull plate still connected wrapped tightly around her horn. It took a while to figure out exactly what was moving through the thorns. How this might have happened makes for interesting conversation.

I n Africa, opportunity knocks loud. A leopard killed a calf on a nearby ranch, a disorganized pack of dogs found it, and I ended up taking the shot originally intended for someone else. • The following year I was hunting kudu when an amazing waterbuck showed up and made me forget about spiral horns.

I t took a long time to find a sable like this. With heavy, 43-inch horns, he is possibly the most beautiful animal I've ever taken. • A great springbok and a 58-inch kudu, my best. I had been watching the ram when the kudu showed up, and the shots came just moments apart.

F ew have been fortunate to take the trophy of a lifetime and share the moment with family. From left: author, wife Kellie, son Ross and daughter Keni. Taking my family on safari is simply the best thing I've ever done. • Ross' chance came two days later, and he did everything right.

A t 51 3/8 inches wide, the author's Cape buffalo is the new national record for Namibia. Ross' bull is 48 1/8, and ranks number seven. Both were taken after we closed with bachelor groups in the thick cover common to the Caprivi Strip.

A bighorn permit for Montana's Missouri Breaks is one of the hardest draws in America – and with good reason. Ross drew the tag when he was a senior in high school and took a 40-inch ram. • Keni first hunted Africa when she was 15, taking some great trophies. While her nearly 58-inch kudu is more impressive, this photo with her warthog is priceless.

Gary Hudson was my guide on a grueling sheep hunt in Alaska's Brooks Range. We spent four days climbing several mountains, trying to find a promising Dall's ram. We finally got close, but I decided to pass. • On the way down the mountain, we stopped for a break and spotted a pack of wolves hunting caribou. It almost didn't happen, but my luck changed for the better.

M y best-ever elk, from the Hubble Ranch in New Mexico. Just 28 inches wide, he still scores 355 Boone & Crockett points. Another hunter shot at – and missed – one far larger the next morning. • Keni took this whitetail, her first, early one opening morning on public land near our home in Montana.

Keni had just begun to field-dress her whitetail buck (previous page) when we heard a bugle. Minutes later we caught up with a herd of elk and she shot this bull, her first. She dressed them both, and then we quartered and packed them out. I don't know who was more proud.

This battered desert bighorn ram lazed around near us all opening day, but we thought there was a better one on another mountain a few miles away. After waiting 20 years to draw a permit, I was in no hurry. We finally caught up to that other ram and realized our mistake. It took nearly two weeks to get close to this old warrior again.

swallowed hard and bought it. Reading it again kindled a multitude of desert sheep permit application and rejection cycles, but the chance to hunt mule deer finally came. In truth, it happened by accident.

I called a friend to catch up and asked if he might like to chase deer for a few days somewhere fun. We talked options and almost settled on Wyoming. Then he mentioned Sonora and that he knew of a good place. Two days later our hunting dates were set, but I really didn't believe it was happening until I stepped off the plane in Hermosillo.

Ernesto Zaragoza and his son, Ernesto Jr., are two-of-a-kind. Along with other family members, they steer successful construction and fishing businesses in addition to a hunting operation on their vast ranches. Since they began taking hunters in 1983, their Solimar Hunting Safaris has established a reputation as one of the finest in Mexico. The lands they hunt are so big and wild that each year they receive nine or ten desert bighorn permits in addition to unlimited mule deer, Coues' deer and javelina tags.

Success rates are high, even though most of their hunters are particular, as well they should be. In 2001 a total of 24 Coues' deer hunters took nine bucks that qualified for Boone & Crockett. Every sheep hunter took a big ram and several of the 30 mule deer hunters wrote entry checks and sent them to Missoula.

Maybe they run such a first-class operation because they're dedicated hunters. Ernesto's trophy room is said to be among the finest in North America and Ernesto Jr.'s can't be too far behind. Both gentlemen – which they are, indeed – are riflemen. Several times they uncased fine rifles and offered a handful of cartridges to anyone interested in stepping out back and leaning over a fencepost.

They run two camps with about five hunters in each for three weeks during the January deer rut. Senior runs one and Junior heads up the other. Camp isn't really the right word for the remote, remodeled ranch houses with generators, real beds, hot showers and a chef that ought to be working his magic in Manhattan.

Generally, one hunter or another would work his way down to the beach on the Gulf of California for lunch every day. When a fishing boat would sail by, they would wave them ashore and exchange $10 or so American for the catch-of-the-day. Squid, the famous Guaymas

Bay prawns and all manner of saltwater fish would be served that night, backed by fine wine or a shot of tequila. Usually both. We had steak on the off nights.

Mornings began when someone kicked over the generator and the lights came on. After getting enough breakfast to last a week, each hunter climbed into one of the Jeeps with his driver and guide. After the Jeeps scattered, you wouldn't see another hunter unless the sun flashed off a windshield miles away.

Sometime later when the light came up, the guide would tap you on the shoulder and invite you to join him up top. Standing in back, rifle resting bolt-open on the bikini top, you eased through the cactus flats and occasionally stopped to glass distant hills.

I was assigned to the care of a wonderful fellow named Pancho, and when a gentle double-tap of his finger on the canvas top brought the Jeep to a halt, he would point out deer, coyote, bobcat, sheep, javelina or some other native critter, perhaps even a plant or bug. It took three days before I managed to see a deer before Pancho or Sergio, our driver, spotted it.

Until mid-morning the Jeep would follow faint trails through the desert while we looked for fresh tracks and for fresh deer standing in them. Pancho would double-tap the Jeep to a stop and off he would go, sometimes looking back to give me the Yellow Pages walking fingers sign. I would follow him down an arroyo or over a *loma* until he was satisfied or discouraged – I could never tell. Then it was back to the vehicle.

Once, Pancho decided the Jeep was too far away, so he torched a dead cactus. Black smoke curled into the sky and soon the Jeep was crunching down the trail.

When the sun was high we searched out a shady place. Pancho scratched up wood for two fires – one for coffee and another for burritos with fresh-cut makings from the ice chest that rode under the elevated rear seat. Then it was siesta time, a wonderful custom that ought to become popular north of the border. The afternoon hours were a repeat of the morning, with deer coming out to feed at sundown.

108

Sonora's countryside is an easy place for deer to hide. They are always just steps away from a rock, cactus, bush or hilltop. Almost everything except cactus is the same shade of buckskin-brown. The landscape is colored like it was painted with a spray gun, with the cactus added as an afterthought like shapeless green candles crowded onto a giant brown birthday cake.

We never saw more than a dozen mule deer in a day, and the camp average was about eight. Still, on the second evening there were four wonderful mule deer bucks, two good Coues' bucks, and one or two bobcat pelts hanging in the meat house.

One of the mule deer was exceptional. Chocolate brown antlers more than 30 inches wide forked and forked again with mirrored symmetry. He had appeared in a canyon my friend and his guide were glassing, wandering nowhere in particular and probably just thinking about girls. He stopped less than 200 yards away. One shot, one deer.

The Coues' whitetail my partner shot the next morning was at least as good in relative terms. The heavy-beamed little beauty probably knew the hunters were there, but worked his way through an opening anyway. Then for some reason he slowed, maybe to look back. Another shot, another great deer.

My turn came later. Like every other morning, we drove, glassed, tracked and occasionally passed up a buck, including a wonderful old-timer that had just about everything except a fourth point on one side, in addition to a forkhorn that had to go 30 inches inside.

At one point my guide decided to stop and go exploring. He made a walking motion, so I took off my coat and followed. It wasn't long before I spotted a mule deer doe looking at us from a clump of bushes at the base of a little hill.

Full of myself for finally seeing something first, I gestured to Pancho. As we glassed the cover surrounding the doe, several deer blew and ran out behind us, flashing through tiny openings as they went. Neither of us saw antlers. Looking back at the first doe, we both watched as a little buck came out to join her. Keeping to cover, we worked our way toward the pair.

I don't remember who saw him first, but we both watched as he stepped clear of the deep shadows and moved slowly toward the doe with the sore-footed rhythm of old age. The little buck squirted out of the way to give him room. We had the wind and the doe had stopped looking in our direction. For several minutes we glassed and gestured. With the sun shining head on and because of the thick curtain of cover, we wanted to make sure.

Remembering that Ernesto had told Pancho I was insistent on finding an exceptional deer, I mimed a shot and then a question. He looked again, then nodded.

I held my hands wide apart and turned them palms up to show another question.

"*Vente-ocho,*" he whispered. Then he drew "2-8" in the skin on the back of his hand with a fingernail, and made the shooting motion.

I crawled a little bit to get clear, stayed prone and dialed up the Leupold. After the doe moved away the slack came out of the trigger. The rifle jumped and back came the kettle-drum *thump* of a good bullet strike. The buck turned half around, then went down. Pancho pulled me up. Smiling, he wiped his brow to show relief.

The buck was even better up close, and while Sergio eased the Jeep across the desert floor, we admired the thick beams and wondered about the scars on his back and neck. We dressed and carefully tied him down for the long ride to the ranch house.

Ernesto Jr. heard the Jeep coming and met us at the door. He knew we had a deer or wouldn't be coming in early. Senior had visited that morning and teased him with a photo of a big buck a hunter in his camp had taken the day before. Ernesto and his father have a gentleman's wager on which camp will produce the season's best deer, and that one green-scored more than 200 points. After the dust settled, the other deer beat mine by a couple of inches, but that didn't matter one bit.

Later that afternoon several of us worked across the flats behind the ranch house looking for javelina. I didn't have a Coues' deer tag and my friend's was notched, so when some little warship-gray does broke cover and trotted over a hill in front of us, followed by a buck that seemed twice as big as any brought into

With Thanks to Ernesto, Jack & Mrs. Shirley Evans

camp, it shouldn't have been much of a surprise. As soon as the deer went over the hill we hurried back to get Ernesto, but he never caught up to them.

Jack O'Connor was right about Sonora, and I can't wait to go back.

Originally published in the July/August 2004 issue of Safari *magazine.*

Jocelyn Russell
© 2009

Chapter 14

Accidental Leopard

For me at least, the opportunity to hunt leopards has always come as a surprise. Not for lack of wanting to hunt them. Far from it. Leopards just seem to show up when I'm cross-eyed from looking long and hard for something else.

The first time was in Zimbabwe. Our camp was set above a wide river etching the border of Gonarezhou Park, however you wish to spell it. Hallowed hunting ground if ever there was, buffalo were on our mind. We rolled into camp in time to check rifles with dime-size holes in their barrels, then squared off against a table so heavy with kudu steaks, impala chops and fresh vegetables from one of the country's few remaining gardens that seven of us never made a dent.

Afterward around the fire we played the strange version of African chess common to first nights. Let me explain . . .

While serving multiple purposes, not the least of which is gaining insight as to how his hunter might react when shaking hands with something hairy and scary, the PH very properly directs the conversation to other game that's available, but not already under contract. Trophy fees, to no great surprise, are apt to ebb or flow based on enthusiasm of the reaction.

The PH began, "Might anyone be interested in elephant? Two bulls remain on quota, and the boys are seeing tracks."

A hyena interrupted, hurling vile insults through the darkness. A splash that could be a crocodile or a hippo or a substantial fish echoed right behind.

"Possibly," came a convincingly flat answer, directed more to the fire than the host. "What else is available?"

Ice clinked in several glasses. Another big splash came from the river. Itches were scratched. The PH's wife joined us and set our minds wandering and wondering.

As it turned out, just about every species was available, given the political circumstances in the country. Moreover, pricing seemed on the Scotch side of fair. Before my head hit the pillow I was down for four of the big five, and only four because there was no chance for rhino.

I have never experienced a bad African hunt, and this would be the only one to end largely unsuccessful. We tracked a lone bull buffalo for almost three days and jumped him three times, but never got a clear shot. We never saw lion sign or heard a roar, and the feet of the elephants crossing the two-tracks were small, at least for elephant feet.

My partner, a depressingly lucky man one still cannot help but like, was carried through this game-rich country on the shoulders of angels. He fetched me up one day to take hero shots of his 59-inch kudu, and again the next morning so he could pose with a stunning 28-inch nyala. When he did no better on buffalo, I mustered little sympathy.

With two days left a big leopard tore into each of our baits. It seemed logical to sit for mine that evening, but my malarial PH thought otherwise. After buffalo we would go, stopping only to trim the leopard tree with a young impala ram.

The last morning brought fresh spoor and less impala. We planned to surprise him around sunset, take some fast pictures then drive all night to the airport. Shooting the moon, we passed on 13 feet of crocodile lazing near the bait after reasoning a shot might lessen our chances. Long story short, the leopard was inbound as darkness fell and a hyena kept him away.

My friend's leopard hauled itself up the tree at the last instant, then promptly silhouetted his body against what faint color remained in the western sky. They could hear the truck coming to pick them up before the shot. It was a huge tom, literally beyond description. My PH looked at his feet and remarked that our cat was every bit as big, maybe bigger, according to the tracks. His observation provided as much comfort as winning the popular vote while being trounced in the electorals.

Accidental Leopard

My absolute favorite place in Africa is the Eden Wildlife Trust in Namibia. Run well by Jamy and Rentia Traut, Eden is more than 100 square miles filled with game. What calls me back, in particular, are Jamy's huge kudu. No matter the odds, I always sign up for cheetah, problem elephants or lions, and the leopards that frequent the area. Some of the surrounding properties run cattle, and leopards from nearby Bushmanland sometimes forget their manners and opt for an easy meal.

While he had always hung baits before, after hearing my Zimbabwe story Jamy had them strung through the countryside. If there was a leopard about, it was a vegan, as the baits were only feeding birds when we arrived. Occupied with getting a kudu that would stretch the tape past 5 feet, we ran the hunt to the final day without much thought of things with spots. After dropping us at a promising blind, Jamy returned to camp that last morning to confirm our outbound arrangements. He came back a bit early to pick us for lunch, visibly upset. The story came out through gritted teeth, slathered with frequent apologies.

A big tom leopard had killed a cow on the neighboring farm sometime the previous night, then fed heavily. The farmer knew Jamy had a hunter who was absolutely mad for a leopard, and radioed immediately after following the drag to the covered carcass. Jamy confirmed I would give the leopard a try, and the farmer agreed to round up his dogs and wait for us near the crime scene. We would be there in less than an hour, and Jamy dropped everything to get ready.

As he was pulling out of camp to collect us, the farmer radioed again. Seems he wanted to be sure the leopard was as big as he suspected. Without considering possible outcomes of his actions, he had loaded his dogs in a truck, trundled just down the road and dropped them on the track. Leopards tree, after all, and he could preview. This action proved once again that good intentions do not make up for stupid. Weighted down by a bunch of beefsteak, the perfectly huge leopard did not act according to union rules. Instead, he chose to fight it out on the ground just four minutes into the chase. Seeing his dogs getting the worst of it, the farmer was forced to shoot. Ever the gentleman, he did offer us the leopard anyway.

Jamy's response to that act of selflessness and charity was predictably curt, and I believe he took the news worse than me. The big kudu we managed that night knocked off some of the edge, at least to the point we could laugh about the disaster some months later.

I was supposed to hunt moose in the Arctic the next September, but we scrapped out in the draw. I say we, because a friend and I had plans to film the adventure for his TV show. A quick call to Jamy turned Alaska into Africa – a good trade at that. We agreed to a full bag of plains game for him. I opted for kudu and more kudu, with a side of leopard if one presented itself. A favorite cameraman was assigned to come along, and the network was relieved not to be facing 22 minutes of dead air.

In the year since I'd last hunted in Eden, leopards had overrun the area like misguided college students campaigning for a liberal candidate in closely contested race. Pondering this analogy further, one might naturally conclude the common solution is setting the dog pack after the interlopers. But even dogs have standards. They're reluctant to chase something that whines more than their own litters. While a leopard cannot change his spots – or dining habits once establishing a decided preference for steak tartare – the naïve young liberal will almost certainly do so as soon as utility bills and 1040 forms begin appearing in his or her own name. Still, there is honest pleasure to be had by visualizing Ol' Blue bayed up and tugging enthusiastically on the activist's nose ring.

In the weeks leading up to the hunt, frequent communications with Jamy confirmed a big leopard was on the dole at a bait in Bushmanland. Skinners were making a regular four-hour round trip to keep him coming, and even reported he was comfortable enough with the provisioning to show himself well before dark. Clearly, he seemed destined to be a TV star, if for only a moment. The only problem was that the hunter in camp before us had established first right. No matter; others were about and troubling Elmer Fudd's cows next door. Achieving clarity, Elmer had also agreed he would no longer be hunting *a cappella*.

We landed at Eden's private strip to the news that the Bushmanland leopard, now "my" leopard, was still in possession of his hide. He had apparently decided to stretch his legs for a few days at just the right time, and for long enough that the previous hunter had pulled back to the main camp and taken some wonderful trophies for his trouble. All we had to do was wait for the cat to return, scuttle to the waiting blind and set up the camera. Runners were assigned to report daily, and I could busy myself hunting kudu.

116

Since both of us wanted a leopard, it was agreed that my friend would take his behind the dogs if one showed up. I suppose it's necessary to mention that my particular leopard did return to the bait, exactly one day after the conclusion of our hunt. In fact, he was probably there when we flew over him coming out of Johannesburg. If leopards had thumbs, this one would have no doubt looked up and pressed his against his nose.

Even with the camera in tow, the first days of the hunt were successful beyond the scope of our dreams. Jamy made things look easy. A very good gemsbok bull came first, followed by a boar warthog, blesbok, 55-inch kudu and finally the king of all eland. Even following the line of march, more to untangle camera cords than anything else, I managed a nice gemsbok and a giraffe for the local orphanage. Everyone was shooting well and having a grand time. However, the nightly leopard report was as disappointing as stepping on the bathroom scale after the holidays.

The daily routine was to head out before daylight, swing back for a quick lunch, then hunt until dark. During lunch on day five or six – days in paradise run together – the radio crackled news of a dead calf and fresh leopard tracks. We were on the road in moments, forks left spinning in plates. The dogs were still being herded up when we stormed the rendezvous point.

"Remind me to sell this truck when we get back," Jamy said in absolute seriousness. "My wife will never want to drive it again after what I just did to it."

Five dogs of mysterious heritage were soon loaded into a battered stakebed. We followed, swilling water against the desert heat. Several miles away the driver choked the life out of the engine just shy of the drag trail, a bloody trough pressed deeper than I expected into the blonde sand. Jamy sized up the tracks and without hesitation declared that the owner was a large tom.

The rules of engagement were quickly outlined. The trackers would take point, moving the dogs along the trail until the cat was jumped. At that time, the two forward guns would be chamber-loaded and the hunter would quickly follow Jamy to the front for a shot. The cat would likely tree after a short run. Repeated emphasis was placed on the need to shoot fast but true, and also before the leopard realized people were behind the dogs. Once that happens, it was suggested, attentions might be redirected to ill effect.

My lot in life was to follow the cameraman, mostly to help him navigate the brush without hang-ups, but also protecting him in case things went wrong. Off we went with the enthusiasm of a band of little boys chasing grasshoppers – or maybe bigger boys chasing girls.

We soon found the dead calf, half-eaten and covered with sticks and dirt. Clearly, his last moments on this earth were as pleasant as waking up to discover the woman you are spooning is Rosie O'Donnell. From there, the tracks lined out and we followed, moving in their wake through the thick brush as best we could.

The dogs, clearly not the product of selective breeding, cast about, but the sun had climbed high enough that what little scent there might have been did not seem to register. No one spoke above a whisper.

More than two hours after leaving the calf, the trackers spread out and began circling. It seemed unlikely they had lost the trail, but Jamy translated that there were now two leopards, both toms. For some reason or maybe by pure chance, one had crossed the trail of the other and was now following in its footsteps. We were close behind them, he said, and should now move very deliberately.

Minutes later, and probably because I was last in the serpentine, I was the only one who saw one of the cats break cover. There was no time for a shot. Before I could gain anyone's attention, a tracker kicked up the other leopard, and it was off like a prom dress. Finally showing signs of life, the dogs opened and followed.

Leopards seldom fight it out on the ground when there are big trees to climb, and this place was something of a forest. Still, for reasons known only to the cat, it backed into a hollow and began hooking at the frantic dogs. Jamy quickly set up the sticks for the shot, but the cat was off again before the trigger could break. Fifty yards later he did it again, but dogs were in the way. This time the cat blew the dogs back with a roar and dove into the thickest brush he could find.

Jamy was becoming frantic, and yelling in Afrikaans, the trackers were encouraging someone to do something fast. Another roar came, then a cry from one of the dogs. Jamy yelled for me to come up and shoot if I could, but there was no way to get by everyone on the narrow trail. The leopard quickly bayed again, this time while lying down.

Through my binoculars I could see his tongue lolling. Incredibly, one of the dogs was doing the same thing, no more than ten inches separating their noses. Again there was no shot, and the chase resumed the next instant.

The trackers were shouting at Jamy now, as I later learned, to shoot the cat before it charged through the dogs and jumped on one of us. They were also falling behind us, wanting to put as many guns between them and the cat as possible. Smart guys, those trackers.

The leopard bayed again a dozen yards farther. Conditions were no better, but all had gone to Hell enough that something had to be done. When the cat ran again, Jamy took a shot with his .458 Winchester Magnum. The big bullet shattered a thick limb just in front of the muzzle and did nothing but give slight encouragement to the dogs.

Deciding it was finally time to join the party, I ran past the cameraman through an open area, keeping a careful eye on the other rifles and the leopard. Luckily, I got the angle.

Jamy could see I would probably have a shot and corrected his course to intersect me. One of the trackers beat us there with the sticks, but I centered a swatch of yellow hide on my own.

"Shoot! Everyone is clear!" Jamy yelled.

I did, too. The cat ran a few more steps. We moved with him, and I hit him again after the dogs cleared. This time he rolled completely over and was still.

My friend piled up behind me to cover the cat while I topped off my magazine. Ever the gentleman, he congratulated me roundly on my success, even though the cat would have been his first leopard as well.

After making sure the leopard was dead, Jamy translated something one of the trackers was trying to tell me. Laughing, he shook his head and relayed, "This is not the leopard that killed the calf. That leopard is bigger and they want us to take him as well."

I told him to tell the tracker that I was more than in agreement, and that my friend still wanted a leopard for himself. That made him smile, but that leopard never came back to give us a chance. Maybe my bad leopard luck had rubbed off on him.

Originally published in the July/August 2007 issue of Safari *magazine.*

Chapter 15

Bugles & Broken Dreams

There is a Christmas in July. A genuine look-forward-to-it Christmas like those long ago that held promise of a first BB gun or maybe even a deer rifle. Preparations begin in early spring, about the time the snowline sneaks back up the tallest mountains and bears pop out of their dens because they're as hungry as, well, bears. The hard part is never-minding away the odds. Get past that, and all you really need to do is scratch out a few numbers on an application, write a check and stuff them both in an envelope. Then you wait for the Arizona elk draw like the river card when you're all in.

Just after the smoke clears from Independence Day fireworks, a few lucky hunters will hold a tag that gives them the opportunity to hunt the biggest elk in the land. Most get their money back and console themselves with thoughts of next year. At worst, taking a chance at the draw builds a quality that old men still call grit, a reasonable risk since some of those tags get wrapped around an antler as thick as a Dixie Chick's ankle.

As in most elk country, Arizona's best hunts come during the rut. Those falling later in the year are not really much better than offered by other states, although there are certainly fewer hunters. All tags issue through a draw, and odds predictably reflect both trophy potential and the type of hunt. If you don't want to worry about deadlines and picking the best areas, there are several application services that will carry your water.

John McClendon owns one of them, it so happens, but that is not the reason to hunt with him if you get lucky. John is hands-down one of the best elk guides alive today. Elk and hunting them are his life and passion. He is out there among 'em months before the season begins, searching out big bulls for his hunters. Want proof? Guys who pay six figures for the state auction tag almost always hire him, and in 2005 one of his archery hunters arrowed a bull that grossed 432 and netted 414 typical. After the judges' panel has its say, the rack will likely be the new sharpened-stick world record. Personally, John is an accomplished archery hunter with two bulls crowding 400 on his wall at home. He is also very good with a videocamera, and his Northstar Video Productions hunting films are a must if big elk haunt your dreams.

For the last 20 or so years I had applied for early rifle and muzzleloader elk hunts in Arizona. I had been drawn three times and hunted with McClendon twice. Our first time together was during a drought that had dramatically reduced antler growth. I had a rifle permit in the very best unit, and we bugled in several bulls that would have gone into the very high 300s any other year. We hit it hard and let bulls as big as 360 walk away, hoping against all reason that one monster was out there. If he was, we never found him, but we did cut the coyote population down to thin.

Like most states, Arizona posts drawing results on their Web site. Being generally resentful of the way technology has disturbed the natural order of things, I liked it better when good news arrived in the mail in tangible fashion. Swallowing some pride along with a tall rock shandy, I checked the 2005 results while hunting in Africa and learned I had pulled a chance at a big bull, this time for one of the muzzleloader hunts.

Less than a minute later, an e-mail to my wife asked quickly about her general health and well-being, and then requested that she call McClendon and book the hunt. He quickly confirmed we would hunt together for the six-day season.

Rain kept up during the rest of Arizona summer, so feed was everywhere and antler growth was strong. All looked promising when I unloaded at the camp set well back from the hunting area below the Mogollon Plateau in Tonto National Forest. John would be along as soon as his last archery hunt was wrapped, so guide David Rhodes met me at the end of the pavement for lunch. He had been scouting for three days and had seen several bulls in the mid-300s. Every one of them had been bugling hard. After settling in, we split up to look at one last promising mountain that afternoon, but neither of us saw elk.

Hunting elk in the Southwest is different from other places. Water is all-important and the days are hot. There is a distinct morning and evening opportunity, and not really much else. The animals bed during the heat of day, and chances are good that the best bulls will be herding cows. Instead of stumbling into them in the thick timber, you just find some shade and nap with them, waiting for their bugles to start back up when the sun begins to slide down the edge of the sky.

On opening morning we started hiking into a wilderness area about two hours before shooting light, hoping to get a good look at a bull David had seen a couple of days earlier.

"He's a straight six, big and bladed," David said, responding to my predictable inquiry. "I don't think he's broken up and looks to be about three-seventy."

Finding a bull that doesn't have a crewcut from fighting is something of a chore. With a bull-to-cow ratio approaching one-to-one, Arizona bulls brawl like sailors on shore leave. Snapped tines and main beams along the trail become a daily reminder.

L ight came up as we switch-backed the last part of the mountain. Things were quiet where the bull had herded his cows around two mornings earlier. Topping out, we spotted a cow feeding through a big juniper thicket. After a time we called, but there was never an answer and no other elk appeared. We moved on when a bugle whispered from somewhere ahead. Through the wind we heard it several more times, and it brought us to a ridge between two heavily timbered bottoms where we stopped to listen and took on the first water of the day.

It was warming already, and the cold water had a welcome taste. The bugle came again from somewhere below. It was high, short and somewhat unsure. A shifting of tan soon betrayed a raghorn in a stand of big pines. He stepped into an opening as the bugle from the other bull sounded and stopped him like he'd hit the end of his leash. This one was low, throaty and ended with a series of grunts that would put Howard Dean to shame.

We moved down the ridge to a point opposite and above the owner of the big voice. Setting up in good cover with several shooting lanes, we pulled on facemasks. I capped the rifle and spun off the secondary safety.

"Ready?" David whispered?

I nodded, and he hit his bugle.

From somewhere below the bull hammered back, then tore into a tree to press his point. David chirped on the cow call. Moments later his bugle flirted back again, this time much closer.

A trail of sorts ran over the crown of the ridge and toward the sound, so I swung in that direction and brought the rifle to my shoulder. David cupped his hand and threw the sound of the cow call behind us, and the bull pushed his way into the clearing 30 yards away. My thumb never pushed the safety forward, and I almost laughed out loud.

Weeks before this bull had been a grand 6x6, certainly a 350 and maybe much more. Today, he carried nothing but two 50-inch main beams with eye guards. His bays were broken short on both sides and every point above them was snapped off jagged at the base. It looked for all the world like a chainsaw had run down both sides of his rack. We got a pretty good look at him, too, because he walked by at about 8 feet, eyeballed us for a moment and kept on after the errant cow.

We gave him some time and then crawled out of the cover to plan our next move. Before we had a chance, the big bugle sounded again from down the mountain. The bald bull was a satellite, not the boss, so we set up again for another chance. The bugle and the cow call brought answers, but always from the same place.

"He's bedded," David said. "We'll try to find him this afternoon."

There was a good spot nearby where we could look down a steep hillside into the canyon. More importantly, it promised shade. We sprawled, lunching and napping and waiting for hours. Occasionally the bull would bugle from his bed, nothing serious, just clearing his throat. An hour before dark he went after a tree.

David was on him with the bugle right away. He said something unkind to start a war of words, and we followed along as the bull pushed his herd straight up the bottom to higher ground. Cover was thick and we could not see him, but he was lined out.

Using the superior cognitive skills commonly found in both politically conservative *Homo sapiens* and the plots of old Western movies, we hurried ahead and took up a position in some big rocks. Effectively and literally, we headed him off at the pass. It was a perfect setup, rifle rest and all, but he turned off somewhere below and drove his cows away into the coming darkness. We picked our way down through the rocks and rattlesnakes that only seem to matter when the elk are not calling. Back at the truck, I promised myself to carry more water the next day.

We were in the same big rocks just after daylight the next morning. Two bulls were bugling hard somewhere below. We slipped toward them and gained more of the wind. A squeak on the cow call soon had one of the bulls coming hard. I saw the top of his horns and a little of his legs at 40 yards as he circled closer, then lost hope as he caught the wind and moved away. We took off after the other bull, pushing him until we heard the two distinct syllables of a blackpowder rifle's *ka-pow* in the distance. There was nothing to do but stop and wait.

David thought we were in a good place, at least as good as any, so lunches came out. We took turns napping and watching, but nothing showed other than a few of the small local whitetails.

"Ever hunt them?" David asked, staring after them.

I told the truth, that I just couldn't get excited about making a trip for these guys with so many big bucks walking through my yard in Montana.

We rolled out from under our cluster of ponderosa pines when we figured the elk were starting to think about dinner and took off in no particular direction. I suspected we were going to find an overlook into the main canyon. Not yet even thinking about elk, I ducked under a low limb and ran into David's pack. I followed him as he went to his knees and crawled behind a big tree. He looked through his binoculars for a moment, then motioned me forward and to ready the rifle. I heard the videocamera coming to life just over my left shoulder.

A good sign, I thought, and pulled up my face mask.

Not far ahead I saw a tree shaking, but the bull was hidden. We watched for a time, and then one chirp from the cow call had the bull inbound. He slid to a stop like a baseball player at 8 yards, and then bugled straight in my face. Slobber flew end-over-end in ropes, and after his bugle closed out with a double chuckle, I could hear his labored breathing mixing with mine. His beams were heavy, certainly as thick as any bull I'd ever seen. The six points on each side were long and perfectly matched. Anywhere else, he was a keeper. At 340 and in the Arizona rut, we let him parade around until we were all tired of it and let him move away. He was the last elk of the day.

John met us in camp that night, ready to go and still excited about his hunter's bull from the previous week that went on to become the new Pope & Young world record. He had plenty of photos, of course. David had to leave after the morning hunt, so John made plans to look over another area and give us one last chance together.

We were up at 3:30, driving to a high point that held a water tank. After downhilling the better part of a mile to the head of a serious canyon, we immediately spotted several bands of elk. I managed to sort through two groups, satisfied that neither held a really big bull. David's attention was on another herd in deep shade farther off. Finally, I understood.

"We need to go look at that bull. I caught him broadside, just for a second, but his main beams go forever."

There was a mile to go and we had covered half of it when a bugle drifted over the ridge just ahead. It wasn't much, but the one that hit it right back was full of rumble. We came out above the bulls in a few minutes. Two raghorns were on either side of a monster working his cows up the far side. He was in range, but I was on him with binoculars first to be sure. When he finally turned my heart fell into my boots. His left brow tine ran down the bridge of his nose past the tip, and then turned up. The other brow had been snapped off at the base.

"That bull was three-ninety before that point got busted," David whispered. Looking him over, there was no reason to argue.

We left them there and kept working toward the other bull. It took a long time to find him, but finally he moved through an opening. What I saw made me want to cry. His left side wore eight or maybe nine points and several looked to be crowding 2 feet long. None of that mattered, because his right main beam was snapped off clean at the royal. Days or weeks ago he would have scored well over 400. It was a long walk back to the truck.

The next morning found John and I in another part of the area, above a river that held elk during the early summer months. We didn't see anything other than some great country, but John called a friend who lived in the area and turned up a good lead. He had been out that morning and spotted two good bulls not far away. We looked for them that night, struck out, and agreed to try again that next morning.

Climbing to the top of a little hill, we listened and waited for daylight. As the light grew stronger, John pointed out a big bull working along a far ridge. He was alone, and since there was no wind, maybe close enough to hear a call. John gave him all he had, and the bull answered right back, changed course and came our way. We had plenty of time to look him over. Eight on one side and nine on the other, including the devil points on his brow and a fork at the end of a main beam, he was about 360 only because of a narrow spread and three points that seemed to have missing tips. With a more typical spread he would have gone almost 380. After four days full of badly broken bulls, I didn't care about spread.

We sat up in some cover that offered two good shooting lanes, and then John went to work. He called the bull out with the arrogance of a rock star, and then teased him with cow calls. Every time he called the bull would answer right back, and occasionally we would catch a glimpse of him coming in through the trees. At the last moment he skirted around the shooting lanes and moved to gain the wind. His next bugle was going away. John moved away as well, bugling and cow calling. He went several hundred yards up the mountain, then ran back down and cow-called again to suggest the herd had separated. It worked, and the bull's bugles came closer.

He cleared the juniper at 80 yards, turning broadside. I waited until his near front leg stretched forward, squeezed the trigger and heard the thump of the Barnes bullet. The blue-gray smoke whipped away in the wind and I saw him fall. John came down the mountain, wondering what had happened. I pointed down the shooting lane to the bull and thanked him for the great work. After pounding another charge home, we climbed down to get a closer look. There was no disappointment.

Getting him out took enough doing that it stretched into the next day. While we packed the bull and loaded camp, we talked about John's dream to hunt Africa and of course, next year's Arizona draw. Like always, both of us would be applying early and then waiting through the first months of summer to see if our Christmas would come early.

Originally published in the March/April 2007 issue of Safari *magazine.*

Jocelyn Russell
© 2009

Chapter 16

Ross' Bullet

The buzzing alarm tore me from a dream I probably should not have been dreaming and when I reached across Kellie to turn it off, she barely rustled. I pulled on the pile of wools waiting at the foot of the bed and then glanced out the window. New snow rested on the pines and the sky seemed to still be overcast. I would need to chain up to make it to the top of the mountain, but that would be a small price to pay. The elk would still be there, near where I had watched them last night through the spotting scope until they disappeared in the darkness. Three were bulls and one of them was big. With a two-hour walk and a little luck, he might just come home with me.

Moving downstairs, I let out the dog and threw together some breakfast. I forced it down, knowing it would make the climb a little easier. Before picking up the pack I slipped into the kids' room. Keni was still, sleeping as only babies can. I lifted her pink blankets and softly kissed her temple. Her only reaction was a faint wiggle in the ever-present pacifier. After tucking her back in, I crept past a company of watchful stuffed animals to the bed where Ross slept, knowing he would insist on coming along if I woke him. Together, we had taken a good whitetail buck two weeks before. He helped me dress it out and pack it down the mountain long after dark, just to make sure I wouldn't be scared. Then he proudly announced to anyone who would listen that we had killed the biggest whitetail buck that ever lived. Two sets of grandparents heard the tale later that night during much-too-long phone calls. Only 3, hunting was already a big part of his life.

I smoothed his rumpled covers and pushed him toward the center of the bed. Kneeling beside him, I stroked his soft brown hair, and whispered my plans for the day and told him how much I wished he could go. He didn't stir. I kissed his forehead and slipped out the door to the garage.

After kicking the Jeep over so it could warm and remembering that I needed extra shells, I opened the box where Ross had carefully placed the rounds we'd loaded together before season. Nesting in one of the slots was a bright yellow plastic bolt about three inches long. It took a moment before I realized it was Ross' "bullet." Originally part of a tool set from his grandpa, it fit down the muzzle of his toy rifle and quickly became a bullet. Ross was fond of snapping the trigger, then grabbing the bullet and throwing it at the target. Teeth marks showed the dog also enjoyed the game. Ross picked on her because she was the only big game animal that frequented the family room, a fact Mom made clear one day when Ross stalked his baby sister.

That bullet meant the world to Ross and it being there was no accident. From the time he was little, Ross would often put something that belonged to him in my briefcase, suitcase or pack so he could in some way go with me. He always did this on his own. Their discovery always filled me with pride. Ross put his bullet with mine because it was the natural order of things as he saw them. His bullets should be with mine, because he was supposed to go hunting with his dad. I toyed with the yellow bolt a bit longer, recalling some of the good times we'd already shared and hoping for many more in the future.

The Jeep idle kicked lower, signaling it was time to go. I put the yellow bolt in my pocket for luck and climbed in, understanding how my dad must have felt about leaving me home when I was little and lived to hunt with him.

I didn't find the elk. I hunted hard, too, climbing and glassing and searching for tracks in the cold, deep snow. Each time I thought of giving up, I looked at the yellow bolt and remembered how it felt when I was the one too young to go hunting and then imagined how Ross might be feeling today. It was long past dark when I got back to the Jeep.

Ross' Bullet

I was miles down the road when it hit me. When my generation was still young, nothing stood between us and hunting with our fathers except an extra gun, a few shells and a license. Today was different. Everywhere I looked, from news reports to voting booths to courthouse steps, there were people who wanted to stop hunting, the privilege I had shared with my father and now was just beginning to share with my own son. It was no longer possible to stay out of the fight.

After dinner, Kellie and I played with the kids and finally slipped them into bed. Explaining that I had work to do, I started a pot of coffee. While it brewed, I found my checkbook, some paper and a stack of envelopes and stamps. After pouring a cup of coffee, I started a list of letters to write – politicians, the media, corporations and conservation groups. With that yellow bolt clinched in my hand, I was going to do something to protect my little boy's dream.

Originally published in the April 1991 issue of Bugle *magazine.*

Jocelyn Russell
©2009

Chapter 17

The Gift of Africa

I remembered hearing the song for the first time. It was during the heat of my 15th summer and I was her age almost to the day. Back then it sounded different, not clean and clear and perfect like it did in the split headphones that connected us to each other and the thunder from the tiny, shiny disc.

That first time it had battled through the cracked radio speaker hiding somewhere in the dusty metal dashboard of my '63 Rambler. That afternoon I bought the 8-track album at Green's Drug Store and played it until the deck hanging under the ashtray/ammo storage drawer died and became a Saturday afternoon .22 target.

To mourn this passing I took $2.25-an-hour-money earned in an apple orchard, replaced it with a cassette player and bought the album again. This time it was a record for bootleg taping because I figured to have already contributed enough money toward the band's rehab.

I still play that record on an old turntable now and again, and Keni loves that song today like I have since it made me press hard on the footfeed, crank down the window and sing along.

She marveled innocently when I told her about surviving two or maybe even three concerts by the band.

"Really, Daddy? Can we go see them someday?"

I squeezed her hand harder and told her I hoped we could, for it never mattered what we did together. Still, this particular thing we were doing was a pretty big do, flying to Africa for her first safari.

Born a Hunter

Keni's just-graduated-from-high-school brother slumped hard against her shoulder. Days before, Ross had tossed his cap so high it had yet to come down. Sleep had been scarce for him lately but he somehow found time to pack, kissed his pretty girlfriend goodbye and jumped into the truck I had aimed at the airport with the sole-purpose enthusiasm of a bird dog on that first magic October Saturday morning.

The trip was really his graduation present, at least that was the proffered excuse. He wanted his new first name to be Doctor, and I thought this a fitting show of approval and support.

Mom book-ended the pair from the far side, trying to stay awake and wondering how she was going to survive the 18-hour flight from Atlanta to Johannesburg. In the headphones, Don and Glenn kept jamming while Hell froze over.

I couldn't help but think that God would damn me for taking my children there, for Africa would surely be the full and complete ruination of their lives. Nothing comes close, yet holding other experiences up in hopeless comparison is as unavoidable as the envy from those who have yet to fly the Atlantic against the sun with rifles checked in baggage.

Africa is the trump card of hunting. It is so much better than everything else, even everything else combined, that hunters who have gone learn not to bring it up in polite conversation with the less fortunate. Sharing an Africa story with someone who can only recount a weekend deer hunt close to home is too much of a gut punch. A friend should no more do that than tell a long-married buddy about the blonde starlet he nailed the previous weekend. Africa might even be worse, if only because it is somewhat more customary to share pictures.

Everyone held up pretty well over the water and the ironic two-hour hop backtracking to Windhoek. Namibian customs made us feel as welcome as a crooked politician at a union rally and our gun permits were quickly stamped.

Jamy Traut was there as we bumped through swinging doors, pushing carts heaped with gun cases and duffel bags crammed with khaki clothes and maybe 50 soccer balls for all the children of Eden

134

– the wonderful place where we'd be hunting. We stood still for proper introductions, then crammed and stomped and stuffed everything into two waiting trucks.

I offered Kellie the front seat. "Let the kids trade," she said, smiling motherly. "I want to watch their faces."

This was my third hunt with Jamy, which more than anything else stands as testament to the quality of his operation. He grew up in Eden, a land returned to the most natural, undisturbed state as is possible, primarily for the benefit of wildlife. Others properties share that goal, but fortunate circumstance has allowed Eden not only to operate differently, but to succeed.

Hunting pressure is light. More often than not, just one party at a time is on the property. If that means just one hunter, no one seems to mind. Quality, be it trophy or experience, is the focus. You hunt Eden not as a guest or a friend, and certainly not as a client. You own the place. The food is good and the tents are clean. Soft beds, hot water and cold drinks are always waiting.

At Eden, mindlessly twiddling the first spent cartridge of the safari and gazing into an evening's young fire while a cold rock shandy beads up your glass is a perfect happiness. It's the place where my soul found a home.

Windhoek was soon far behind and animals began to appear. A warthog and her three little ones were first, then a kudu cow and not long after a fine young bull with spiral horns shining in the setting sun. All marveled.

When we pulled into camp, eland, waterbuck, wildebeest and kudu bumped and tumbled away from the waterhole.

Sleep did not come easy, or maybe we just put up a good fight. The sound of Africa's animals splashing in the water and blending with the laughter of our children from their nearby tent is something Kellie and I will never forget. It was better than any Christmas morning.

We rallied for breakfast before first light, scooped up a battery of rifles and drove several miles to a shooting area. Ross and Keni claimed positions they would never relinquish, standing just behind the cab next to Jamy in the open bed of the Hi-Lux. Kellie and I rode just behind on a second bench seat. It was quite chilly, but no one seemed to mind.

Ross fired first from the bench, his Kimber .300 WSM pushing 180-grain Barnes XLC bullets through the target in the same place it did back home.

Keni confirmed her Kimber .308 Winchester just as quickly, and I finished up with a new .325 WSM just in case. Thinking it a good time, we paused to discuss the morning plan.

There was something of a loose agreement between brother and sister as to who would shoot what first. They worked it out somewhere over the Atlantic even though I had been prompting them to do it for several months. Ross had first pick, predictably kudu. Keni opted for a zebra. Order was then given to springbok, impala, warthog, gemsbok and whatever else opportunity provided.

I f it were possible to choose a day of my life to live over again this would surely be it. The animals came out in royal welcome and I saw Africa again for the first time through the eyes of my family.

Keni pointed at a hornbill and, being of the *Lion King* generation, screeched "Zazoo!" in a little-girl voice I had not heard in years. Minutes later she grabbed Ross by the arm and frantically pointed and jumped as "Pumba" trotted across the road just ahead. Just then something got in my eye.

Ostrich paced the truck like Wyoming antelope and giraffe peered down through the treetops. Kellie noticed some vultures resting in a bare tree, outstretched wings taking heat on the dole from the rising African sun.

"What we gonna do?" she mimicked in a low, Limey voice. "I dunno. Whatchew wanna do?"

Questioning looks prompted her to remind that before *The Lion King* there was *The Jungle Book*.

A luggage rack of sorts extended over the cab, and somewhere in the crosshatch of guns and gear was my rifle. Being in Africa without a rifle is not right for many reasons, but it was there mostly because I hoped to stumble over one of the cheetahs that frequently hunted Eden.

I suppose it should not have been a surprise when, 30 minutes into the hunt, we rounded a corner and spotted four of them crossing the road in the distance. We gave them time to settle, then slipped along their tracks. They led us in a big circle, finally pausing in an opening almost long enough. As my safety slipped forward, the big one snapped his tail and disappeared into the thorns.

"Maybe tomorrow," Jamy offered in genuine condolence. "Thankfully, the truck is just there. Water?"

In minutes we were moving again.

Jamy soon separated a kudu bull from the thorns, one that looked better than the first two or three dozen seen in the opening half of morning.

"Who's up first for a kudu?" he asked rhetorically, knowing well the answer.

Ross hurdled from the truck. I handed down his rifle then followed with the videocamera at full port. Kamati, the driver/tracker and one of the finest men I've ever known, set the course.

Working slowly through the brush, we caught up with the bull and another. They needed another year, so at Ross' call we backed away. The decision was fortuitous.

Not far away was one of the busiest waterholes in Eden. We parked downwind and since no one wanted to be left behind, all six of us filed along a faint trail. Approaching the water, Kamati slowed, dropped to a crawl and finally went belly-down to work his binoculars under the brush. Jamy joined him, then turned to the young hunters and whispered, "Gemsbok."

Gesturing for us to stay behind, Jamy crawled forward with Ross. Through binoculars I followed their progress. Ross edged just ahead. He slowly worked the bolt, took a wrap on the sling and pushed his elbows into the sand.

The shot never came. Instead, Jamy tapped his leg and pointed to the right. Glassing frantically, I tried to follow, then something big and gray moved through an opening.

"Kudu. Big kudu!" I whispered to the girls.

I swung over to Ross and picked up his outline just as the rifle jumped into his shoulder and a puff of dust from the muzzle blast twisted away in the breeze. The sound of the shot came, and just after, the thump of the bullet hitting hard.

A spent brass cartwheeled, flashing as it caught the sun. They stayed still for a bit, then crawled out of sight.

Kamati soon motioned us forward. Coming into the clear we saw them standing over two-and-a-half curls of kudu, the kind of bull that brings hunters to Eden and makes their knees wobble when they see it. If someone had to judge a happy contest just then, it would have been impossible to pick a winner.

We hunted our way back to camp and lunched there under noted joint protest.

"We only have eight hunting days, dad," Ross reminded me politely.

"How soon can we get back out there?" chimed Keni. "I'm ready."

To calm things, I told them we would not be in camp more than an hour. Sitting in the shade, we watched the daily parade coming to water. An exceptional waterbuck marched by at 20 yards, guarding his harem from younger bulls that worked the perimeter like teenage boys at a topless beach.

Kudu came and went, along with a warthog with teeth like the Grim Reaper's scythe.

"After the kids get theirs, I want one of those," said Kellie. "Think Jamy will mind?"

I out-loud supposed he would not.

During the drive from Windhoek, Jamy spoke of two exceptional kudu and trying to get a shot at them for weeks. As with some of Eden's largest bulls, they were both a golden color, rather than the more traditional Confederate gray.

When he suggested we spend the afternoon watching for one of them from an elevated blind, it didn't take long to agree.

"Also," he added unnecessarily, "there is a big warthog nearby that might go fifteen inches. I would like to give him a try as well."

We should have seen it coming. When Keni climbed into the blind that afternoon she had yet to hang her first game animal on the wall. As with all things in her self-assured, take-no-prisoners life, she had been unwilling to compromise and take any of the representative deer or elk we had found together during her three Montana seasons.

Instead, she held her tags in trust while we looked for something special. Africa didn't see fit to make her wait. After being in the blind maybe 30 minutes, Kamati's magic eyes found one of the big golden bulls moving through some heavy brush.

The kudu spotted us when Jamy shifted Keni into a shooting position. He turned inbound and stopped, head thrown back. Instead of looking at the bull, I watched the muzzle for signs of nervous movement. It was still.

The shot seemed to take forever, but when it finally boomed, the bull took it hard before flashing away.

We waited for our hearts to settle, took up rifles and walked slowly to where the bull had been standing at the shot. There was blood, and 60 yards away the back half of a dead kudu lay across a little trail. Jamy moved Keni around to be sure, then called us up.

"He is so beautiful," she managed, reaching out with a now-shaking hand. "I love him." Then a "Thank you, Daddy," followed by a kiss.

Keni even remembered to thank her mother, Jamy, Kamati, her brother and eventually everyone in the pickup crew that came to the radio call.

Ross went back for the cameras because something got in my eye again, and after taking pictures, Jamy wrestled a rusted quarter-inch Stanley from the jockey box in the truck. Deep-curled and tall, we spooled out almost 58 inches before reaching the tips.

"Warthog?" Jamy asked me quietly, nodding toward the blind.

I shook my head. "Zebra in the big open areas," I had to reply, because nothing but watching the sunset from out there could make the day more perfect.

At daylight we were back on the truck, searching for gemsbok and impala but mostly, I suspected, for the quartet of cheetahs. Somewhere along a road that cut the top of a miles-wide northern Kalahari dune, Jamy found something about a single track among thousands that was to his liking.

After quietly discussing it in Afrikaans with Kamati, Ross was asked unnecessarily if he would like to try eland tracking.

"Several old bulls crossed here not long ago. Kamati thinks we may catch them, as the wind is right."

Smartly, we all shed coats. Keni asked if she should carry her rifle.

"Yes," I replied. "With your luck, an albino elephant with hundred-pound tusks will charge, and I have no doubt you will drop him with just one shot. Besides, I want a rifle near in case we run into those cheetahs again."

Less than two hours later Jamy and Ross made the final approach on an old eland bull with 36-inch horns. Ross took him clean with a single shot, his rifle resting on Jamy's shoulder.

"That part made me nervous," he said later.

A couple of impala gave us the slip, so we had at some birds with the 12-gauge pump. Ross liked kicking up those big flocks without the handicap of a plug.

The days blurred together. Keni dropped her gorgeous zebra stallion at over 250 yards and later a very good blue wildebeest at almost the same distance.

Ross took the same pair, then a giraffe at the request of the local orphanage and some more animals for the Eden meat locker.

Keni caught up with a huge springbok that she just had to have, then made a terrific running shot on an old boar warthog. She borrowed her brother's rifle for her last shot of the hunt and killed an ostrich at 320 yards.

Ross shot a 23-inch impala Father's Day morning. Kellie never had a chance at a warthog, but it didn't seem to matter one bit.

We thought time had run out for gemsbok, but after stretching the hunt until the last possible moment, Jamy and Ross put it all together in grand fashion. Within two hours I hurriedly took pictures of him with a 15-inch springbok, a Rowland Ward blesbok and a pair of gemsbok.

To keep our schedule we had to rush goodbyes, which in retrospect was something of a blessing. As we drove out of camp, a hornbill flew across the road and landed on top of a camelthorn tree.

Keni rolled down her window, then yelled back at him, "Bye Zazoo. We'll all be back to see you again."

140

The Gift of Africa

I had little doubt, as always, that she was right. Africa had become part of my family, casting its spell on them as it had on me years before. Once that happens, you can't help but return, and I wouldn't want it any other way.

Originally published in the August 2007 issue of Safari *magazine.*

Chapter 18

Counting White Sheep with the Gray Dog

The three of us must have looked crazy. It surely would have appeared that way, at least to anyone watching us pacing back and forth in the little saddle. Being that far north in Alaska's Brooks Range and almost to the top of one of the taller mountains thereabouts, the chance of another hunter being within 20 miles was about as good as any of us getting warm and dry.

Camp was 5 miles away, half of that through a wide valley braided by a meandering river. When we waded it, the cold, blue water often came above our knees, even though we avoided the deeper pools by probing ahead with walking sticks. Our elevation was hard-gained on the slick slides and steep, grassy faces common to the Arctic. We had been hunting a white ram for three days and had yet to get a good look at his head. I hoped that would happen while I had ten toes left to count.

A dark August storm caught us at the foot of the mountain and we climbed into its teeth. Soaked through with water running down our backs, we were quickly chilled to the bone each time we stopped to rest. Every step was more uncertain, and shifting packs made anything other than slow, deliberate steps dangerous. The storm system had grounded outfitter Jerry Jacques for days in his base camp several drainages away, and the prospect of a broken leg followed by a long wait for help was an honest excuse for walking slowly and carefully.

Clouds filled the saddle where guide Gary Hudson thought we might finally be able to get close to the solitary sheep. Finally there, all we could do was throw our packs under some rocks and pace back and forth on little trails, hunched over to prevent the ram from seeing us before we saw him if the wind managed to tear a hole through the fog.

My trail was 13 steps end-to-end, and I counted them for hours trying to get warm. Several times I left the trail and crawled through the rocks to the spotting scope, lifted the garbage bag cover and wiped the moisture from the lenses, hoping to pick up a living white spot from hundreds of white rocks and snow patches in the high basin. I don't remember ever being that cold.

While flying over to check on us several days before, Jerry had spotted the ram standing in the middle of the river, certainly a strange place for a Dall's sheep to be. The ram was big, Jerry said, and I wished as I paced that it had found the river valley more to its liking.

Jerry told me to grab some gear while there was still enough light to fly. We tried to make it but ran out of light and had spent that night on top of a mountain under the wing, waking up surrounded by dozens of sheep. After finding nothing of interest, we flew down into the valley and made a new camp.

Jerry flew in Gary later that day. He introduced himself as "Gary, but you can call me Gray Dog," then set about making camp while Jerry and I off-loaded the Cub and dodged herds of caribou moving up the gravel bar that barely doubled as a landing strip. Jerry dropped off packer Zane Birkley later and we were three.

Clouds covered the mountains the first day, but we hiked several miles up the river with side trips into the foothills, glassing for the big ram. We found him near the time that most people were sitting down for dinner, but he was in the shadows. From three miles we could tell he was good, but not if he was good enough.

The next day we saw him again even farther away, moving over a high ridge. Light was better, but we couldn't get the big glass on him before he walked out of sight.

Sheep hunting is mostly hope and sweat, so that night we decided to give him one last try. Up the mountain was the plan, rain or shine, until we could run a mental tape around his curl and know for sure.

Otherwise, we would give up on him and hunt the rest of our time in other areas. We left at first light and climbed into the rain. The weather changed for the worse.

Late that afternoon the clouds lifted enough so we could see across the basin. White spots appeared and while most were rocks, several sheep got out of their beds and worked their way up the far side. A couple were rams that looked promising until they stood against a solid background and showed tender age.

Options exhausted, we decided to move into the basin since we were there anyway and see if the ram might have circled back below us. We hadn't gone far when a head with golden horns peeked around a rock. Cold forgotten, we tore off the packs and hauled out tripods and scopes one more time. Surely it was him, for his mass showed clearly through binoculars. He watched us right back, and finally turned his head enough to see that while he was certainly a full curl, he wasn't a sheep of dreams. We packed up one last time and slogged back toward the river.

On the way down we stopped on a little bench and finished the last of our food and enjoyed the first sunshine in four days. Caribou shuffled through the valley and there was a tag somewhere in my pack that made them interesting. One of the groups had several big bulls, and while none were as great as those of southern Alaska, they had wonderful white, long-haired necks that shined beautifully in contrast with their dark, wet bodies. We sorted through them, mindful that Zane was along to do the packing and had yet to tie anything to his frame. Then Zane saw a wolf.

Two miles away a white wolf, then a black, then another of each color appeared, working their way down the river. When they discovered the caribou, they paired off and split into cover. I reached for the rifle, hoping for an unlikely shot.

It was a long time before we spotted them again, but one of the whites finally appeared on our side of the valley, gaining elevation while keeping out of sight in a creekbed, no doubt hoping to intercept the dozen cows and calves moving in his direction. Through the spotting scope I could see him crouch low and wait while the caribou filed down a trail leading right past his nose.

When the caribou were only steps away, one of the black wolves rushed them from behind. Panic pushed them forward to the other wolf and they disappeared into the cut with both predators hot on their heels. Seemingly fewer caribou flushed up the other side. The two wolves didn't come out. Things looked promising.

The cut where the wolves disappeared was a good half-mile away, but the wind was right and the contour made a stalk possible. As we quickly whispered strategy back and forth, Zane spotted the other black wolf chasing the herd of big bulls toward us. They were distant enough that there wasn't much of a chance, but I ranged ahead anyway to a cluster of trees. It was more than 600 yards, certainly too far, and the chase took them far beyond the marker trees anyway and down the valley until they were out of sight.

My best chance was to move quickly toward the cut where the first chase disappeared. Gary and Zane would stay behind, directing me with those famous hunter hand signals that seem simple and logical in theory, but can be impossible to understand in practice. Hoping the wolves had made a kill, I figured it might be possible to get in range and do something about it before they spotted me. The plan went flat when both wolves walked back into the bottom and worked their way across the valley and out of sight.

We glassed up nothing for another hour, disappointed and saying little. Taking advantage of the sun, we started looking for sheep across the valley and planning tomorrow's hunt. Sheep came out, but we lost interest in them when the same two wolves walked back into the open and began to cross the river in our direction again.

"Maybe they got one down there after all," said Gary. "They might come back, and if they disappear into that cut, there is still enough light to give it a try."

We went over the signals again, then I took off as soon as the second wolf moved out of sight. Stopping often to glass back at the signal corps, it was an intense 15 minutes before I arrived at a big rock we figured would put me in range. Turning to check the signals, it was a surprise to see Gary point toward the cut as Zane pointed over the valley toward the river at a black spot coming my way. The black wolf that had been chasing the herd of bulls appeared in my binoculars. Stopping in a small opening, it sat down and howled to the rest of the pack. If they answered, I couldn't hear them over my pounding heart.

146

The black wolf was still out of range, but I was between it and where I thought the other two were feeding. Things looked good again. I don't ever remember being as excited as a hunter when I rolled into the rifle. Twisting the Leupold up to 10x and fishing out the rangefinder, I took bearings. The wolf kept coming and stopped near a large, uprooted stump already marked at 325 yards. Holding just behind the shoulder and slightly high, I squeezed the Kimber's trigger. The 168-grain Barnes SLC from the .300 WSM hit hard and the wolf cartwheeled. By the time Gary and Zane had worked their way down to meet me it was almost dark, and together we found the wolf just inside the thick brush.

Jerry flew over as we were skinning, airborne for the first time in four days. After a long, sore-footed walk back to camp, we toasted the wolf with hot chocolate and Mountain House dinners as caribou streamed by to say thanks. We split the last of our candy bars for dessert and headed for the tents when the rain came back.

We hunted down the valley early the following morning, watching sheep come and go on the surrounding mountains. Lots of sheep but no big rams, and I think it was the only day of the hunt when we didn't see at least one with a full curl. What we did see were caribou, including some very good bulls. Late that afternoon we saw a bachelor herd and one stood out from all the rest. Zane allowed how it was time for him to go to work so the stalk was on. The ground was open and rolling, and we couldn't get as close as we wanted. My shot from about 400 staggered the bull, and my trigger broke again just as he started over a contour. I hit him again when he came up the other side and then lost him in the trees.

We found him over the contour. Then we found my second bull. The double was unintended, and my sheep hunt would have been over if it wasn't for the grizzly tag in my pocket. In Alaska, hunters can use a tag for a different species as long as the cost of the tag is greater than one for the species you snap it on. Zane made five trips the next day.

We had two days left and hit it hard, working far down the valley and up another spectacular drainage. We never saw anything that held our interest. The weather generally cooperated, and we made it back to camp in time to cook the last of our real food without flashlights.

Before turning in I took one last look around and noticed a group of sheep working up a mountain 2 miles away. Breaking out the spotting scope, Gary and I looked them over. Four were good, one was better and one looked liked he had it all. We quickly put our gear together and rushed to cut the distance. At last light we got them in the scope. With no chance to get a shot before full dark, all we could do was marvel at horns curling and flaring above the bridge of his nose.

We started after them early, gaining elevation and trusting the sheep would still be on the same side of the mountain. They were. We found them about noon, much higher than the evening before. We climbed, they climbed and the clouds came down, covering them on and off in the perverted game of hide-and-seek that has stolen sheep from sheep hunters for generations. At one point the clouds lifted and the rams were standing far above. It was raining heavily and the glasses kept fogging before we could sort them out. We tried through the spotting scope, holding our rain jackets over it to grab a quick look. Gary guessed the big one at just under 41 inches. I guessed closer to 42. He was amazing either way and neither of us cared who was right about that inch. We kept moving and the clouds crowded lower.

We tried to climb above and cut them off, but the mountain became too steep. Rain poured down in buckets, slicking the rocks as if they were covered in ice. I bent and finally broke an aluminum hiking pole to keep from falling. Out of options, we gave up elevation and came down, worked our way along a creek and then climbed again to where we had last seen them. Waiting it out, the wind came up and got under the fog one last time.

By some miracle, Gary found them again. I sorted out the two big rams, then picked the best. They looked far away, too far, but the rangefinder read 400 and it was now or never. Resting the rifle over my coat, I watched through the scope as the ram lay down, showing only his head. There was no shot, then the fog covered them again.

Full of hope, we cut the distance until hitting a chimney that was impossible to climb. Figuring the sheep were close, we waited one last time, hoping the wind would lift the fog. There was not enough of the day left to pick another route. The rain came down hard and visibility went to nothing. Gary wouldn't quit. He wouldn't even look at me. He didn't say anything when I told him it was time to go back, instead he just picked up his pack and followed me slowly down the mountain.

Jerry was waiting for us, the ceiling having lifted just high enough for him to fly and navigate safely along the river. I threw my gear together and jumped in the plane, planning to meet Gary in camp again that night or the following morning. Zane already had the caribou meat loaded, horns cut and tied to the struts. The wolf rode out in my lap. The weather went bad again after we landed, so Jerry couldn't make another trip to get the others.

A wonderful meal was waiting in the main camp, and resting next to the woodstove were three sheep. One went well over 41, one was more than 40 and the other was 36 because the hunter was in a hurry. A fourth hunter had missed a ram that came over the mountain when the 41 fell, frightened by the shot. That ram was even longer on one side and had a great club at the bottom of his curl on the other. I probably would have missed him, too.

Jerry flew me out the next morning, so I never got to thank Gary in person. By phone that winter, we talked about Africa and how he wanted to make a trip there with his wife. He had planned on retiring from guiding, which he did for fun anyway, but agreed to return for sheep if only I would. In turn, I booked another hunt with Jerry. After all, our ram was still up there.

Gary Hudson loved to hunt brown bear, and agreed to guide a repeat hunter for Jerry the next spring. After their wonderfully successful hunt near Cold Bay, Gary was flying back to Homer where his wife, Nancy, was waiting. A few days digging clams and catching halibut were planned. The weather was good, but the Cub crashed. Gary was killed and the pilot was critically injured.

I was in Africa when Gary's family gathered to celebrate his life. After an exceptional day of hunting, we stood around the fire that June night and raised three toasts under a sky filled with brilliant stars. We toasted the brave soldiers who had fought and died on D-Day 60 years before, then President Ronald Reagan who had just passed, and finally Gary Hudson, fellow hunter and friend. Later, I silently promised to keep my date with the Brooks Range and try again. It won't be the same without Gary, but he will surely be there in spirit.

Originally published in the January/February 2005 issue of Safari *magazine.*

Jaclyn Russell
© 2009

Chapter 19

Andy's Sheep

A convincing argument might be put forth that sheep hunting is as much about color as anything else, at least in the abstract. Get beyond those wonderful, coffee-with-cream horns that turn a complete circle then back on themselves if you are lucky, and sheep hunting takes something from most of the crayons in the big box to illustrate for someone who has never climbed for them.

Shades of blue capture the best as well as the worst of it. In good weather the sky can be so bright it hurts to look at it. You strain for hours through binoculars and tripod-mounted glass with the sun and against it, studying mountains so far away you know you can't get there even if you see sheep on them. The sun burns into the back of your neck more each day, so the first wispy cloud is silently welcomed then out-loud cussed when more follow, flattening the light and making it impossible to glass into the shadows on the nearer slopes you think you can climb by dark.

Two or three times each day and again before zipping up for a few hours' sleep, some robin's-egg-blue Aleve pills shake out into a dirty palm. You throw them back to calm cramping muscles and blistered feet. By the second night your partner is reaching for his helping without asking and by the fourth, the guide no older than your son is bumming regular. "Yukon Skittles," you come to call them, paying as much attention to dosage limits as you did to safe driving reminders on New Year's Eve as a younger man. The bottle stands empty when you leave camp, and you buy another before even thinking of anything else when you get to town. I mean anything else.

Almost all the horses in the string, if you are lucky enough or maybe unlucky enough to hunt from a horse camp, are more or less the same shade of brown, some accented with random white streaks. They are the same brown as the grizzly bears and moose that share the mountains. All are darker than the full sheets of moleskin latticed with white medical tape to hold office-soft feet together so they can be stuffed into wet leather boots each morning.

Two of us were hunting Stone's sheep in Yukon's Pelly Mountains when the deep green leaves of August yield to the bright yellows of September, the meadow in front of the sleeping cabin changing color a little each night. A soft frost came the second week, speeding things along. The days shortened, so much that by the end there was an hour less shooting light, but it didn't matter because everyone was so tired. For the first time I felt the gray in my beard.

The dozen or better rams we looked over each day were different colors. Four drainages west and across a great river, all of the sheep were white. On this side they ran from nearly white to light gray to almost black, at least from a distance. Some had light saddle patches, others dark, and some had color running up their neck and through their cheeks.

History books credit Andrew Stone as the first white man to hunt them, doing that just over 100 years ago and to the south. He took three of them back to the American Museum of Natural History and gave the rest of them his name in possessive form in trade, thereby achieving a measure of immortality. Something over 100 of Stone's sheep are taken each year in the Yukon and maybe twice that in British Columbia. Randy Babala's outfit accounts for about 10 or 11 of Yukon's rams. Almost every one of his hunters is successful. Andy's sheep have become Randy's sheep.

Sheep hunters are a dedicated bunch and sheep hunting is something of a crazed religion. Many of them know Randy as one of the finest sheep guides alive today, maybe one of the best ever. Proof is that he guided a hunter to the new world-record bighorn a few years ago, busting a mark that had stood since 1911. Hunting with Randy is not easy, maybe even an ordeal. Several times each day his blue/gray eyes glared when I coughed or sniffed or stepped in the wrong place. He walked me right into the ground, told me when to take clothes on and off, and how to sling my rifle. Told, not asked. Never said please. The first two days of the hunt were hot, too, well over 80 degrees.

When I climbed into bed that second night, my partner, who was suffering along with me, put it all together. "Dwight, it's just mind over matter. Randy doesn't mind and we don't matter."

The order of the day was eat a giant breakfast, slide a rifle in the saddle scabbard and strap on a pack. Leading the horses until their muscles warmed, we rode when Randy rode, led when Randy led, and stopped to glass whenever we came to new country. Several times the first rams of the day were seen from camp and seldom did it take more than a few hours for the spotting scopes to come out. If any of the rams looked promising we would climb the mountain or ride around it to get closer, for the last few inches of horn that really make the difference are all but impossible to see through heat mirage or at a distance. Once we located some rams, everything we did was quiet and deliberate. Few if any words were spoken until the sheep were in range and it was time to make a decision.

The first days seemed to cover us up with rams. We would spot a band in the distance and work toward them, only to be pinned down by other groups or the odd single along the way. One morning five of them ran by so close we could hear their steps and see them hooking at each other with horns that would be ready for any hunter's wall in two or three more years. We crouched in a little cut, watching. They lounged above for a long time, forcing us to stay contorted in obscene positions on sharp rocks. We thought we were in the clear when they finally fed around the mountain, but they got the drop on us when we peaked over the top and kept us sitting there on more sharp rocks for most of the afternoon. There were plenty of other sheep to watch, so we stayed busy.

The fourth day it all came together. My partner found a ram from the horse trail just 30 minutes from camp and out came three or four spotting scopes. While everyone was pulling on tripod legs, another ram showed himself, looked down on the activity, then calmly dropped his head to feed. Everyone agreed the first ram was something special after he posed on the skyline. Since the "first shot" coin toss didn't go my way, I was at the back of the line when we started climbing.

The sheep had moved around the side of the mountain. We couldn't see them when we topped and it took an hour or so working carefully down the spine before Randy glassed their backlines in a cut below. We used the spotting scope for one last look, but it really wasn't necessary.

Minds made up, Randy worked an amazingly calm hunter into position. The Kimber .270 WSM popped, the sound of bullet to bone came back, the sheep dropped and an old friend was three-quarters done with his second Grand Slam. We worked our way down to the ram together. He was outstanding. A lighter Stone's, gray ran from his rump patch to the front shoulders, yet his head and neck were as white as his all-white cousins to the west and north. His horns didn't pinch in and then flair. Instead, they turned down and up and out in a constant circle that set the tips wide apart.

Several knives pitched in and skinned him for a full mount, then we packed him down the mountain. Randy loaded the head and enough of the meat so he'd have the heaviest pack. Even then he beat us all to camp, leaving the horses for the guide and wrangler to pick up later.

We split up the next day. Randy and the wrangler dragging me along while the others climbed from camp to look for one of the grizzlies that had been leaving deep, wide tracks on the horse trail. We rode for hours through thick brush that seemed there only to give moose cover and tear me out of the saddle. I hung onto the horn with two gloved hands and no hope of using the reins. At least the horse knew what he was doing, pushing through the brush with his head high and simply diving into it when it got thick. If a creek got in the way, he just jumped it. If a tree was in the way, he used one of my knees to break off some branches or push it over.

I was happy to get away from him when we finally tied up at the head of a long valley, ate lunch among the rocks and climbed toward the sun. Smoke from far-away forest fires was settling in, but Randy still pointed out two groups of rams after we reached the top. Searching in a different direction, the wrangler announced that two grizzlies were coming up the ridge our way at a pretty good run.

I wanted a grizzly badly, but these bears were young. They were alternately running and standing to look back, so we hoped a big boar was following with the intent of making one of them a good feed. If he was, we never saw him, but the two little bears seemed determined to run us over. We crawled off the skyline to keep the ridge between us and the sheep, then spread out and waved arms. The bears did not notice and kept coming.

Randy motioned for me to chamber a round, which I did. At maybe 40 yards the lead bear stopped and stood, realizing we shouldn't be there. Dumbstruck as a teenage boy looking at a pretty girl in a prom dress for the first time, he didn't know whether to run way or press his luck. Randy's old dog made the decision for him, tearing down the mountain like a black devil flashing teeth, he chased the bear back the way it came. The same Randy who had days before hissed at me for sniffing my nose yelled repeatedly for the dog to call off the attack, confirming what I already suspected to be the relative importance of everyone in the party.

We bumped the other grizzly an hour later at 30 yards and the dog ran him down the mountain, too. If the rams bedded across the valley saw the chase, they didn't seem to mind. A couple of them looked good, but Randy didn't think there was enough light left in the day to drag me over there and make it back to the horses. I agreed.

Next morning the wind changed. Smoke rolled in thick and we couldn't glass the huge drainages very well, but we went out and tried anyway. Toward evening the wind came up and lifted the smoke. Right away we found rams.

Miles away, the others were watching a big grizzly, trying to figure out how to get to him before dark. They forgot about the bear when a wolf came over the skyline and started their way. Too far for a shot, the hunter charged up the mountain after the wolf got interested in digging for a marmot, leaving the guide to spot and direct. The luckiest and probably the best hunter I know, he's snakebit by wolves. It was gone before he could close the distance.

The next morning was clear. We didn't see any rams before lunch, but a black bear wobbled up the trail and started a pretty good rodeo while we sat and glassed near the horses. A wolverine showed himself, but too far away for a shot.

Early that afternoon Randy did what he does best and sorted out a bunch of rams from some rocks. Riding for several miles, we closed the distance, tied up and started a steep climb. An hour later we were in range. Randy looked hard through the spotting scope, then motioned me over. The glass was centered on a light-colored ram that was bedded facing away. I looked him over from every angle as he turned his head and then stood to stretch and feed. He was a fine ram, probably the best we'd seen, but he didn't take my breath away. We whispered a few words back and forth, and with several days left I decided to pass.

We rode into camp after dark. The others were finishing supper, and between gulps of pie told about jumping a wonderful, flared-horned chocolate ram at close range. He was bedded with a younger ram in some rocks at the top of a small basin, and they stumbled on them while making the final climb to their grizzly lookout.

Later, in the sleeping cabin, a tired voice from the other bunk said, "I think he's broomed a little on one side, if that matters, but he might be the kind of ram you are looking to find."

Taping up my sore feet for another day, I knew where we were going would be on foot, straight up the mountain with no help from the horses.

"How big, really?"

Finally, after doing his election-year best to excuse and qualify and not give a straight answer that I could hold him to later, my friend spit out a number. Good enough for me, I starting taking even things that mattered out of my pack. The next day would be tough.

Three of us started up the mountain early. Heavy clouds were filing in, and by the time we fought our way to the top several hours later, the weather looked serious. If the big ram was still on the mountain, we were surely above him, but that didn't make things easier. The country was rough, and sharp notches were cut everywhere. We crossed slides bad enough to concern the dog and make me think about religion, but the ram might have been in the next chute, and Randy was going to find him with or without my cooperation.

Around noon we felt a few raindrops. Randy crawled to the skyline, then looked back and whispered, "rain gear," with absolute seriousness. By the time we pulled on our pants, we could hear the rumble of the storm. It hit hard. We curled up in the rocks and arranged packs so they took the impact of the hail and sleet. For an hour we couldn't see anything but a gray wall, then it was gone.

Glad to be out of the rocks, we worked along the top to the other side. Nothing. It was late afternoon, and we were above a trail that sided a creek running down past the cabin. Randy asked if I wanted to call it a day. I lied, telling him I wanted to walk farther down the ridge and look into the next basin. Off we went.

I can't imagine what my friend went through that day. Lying in the rocks with his guide on the near side of the next mountain, they had found the ram we were looking for as soon as they topped out. Their hunt that day was for us. They knew where we planned to go first, of course, and thought about coming to look but with all the sheep in the area, they wisely held their position. The moment we came into sight they jumped and waved like two hungry castaways at a distant ship. It took another hour to get to them, as fast as we could go, and they wasted no time in telling their story. The ram was on the next mountain and had just fed out of sight. Five of us took off after him.

I don't remember ever being that tired, and even felt that way after Randy looked back and told us he could see the rams. After straining through the spotting scope for several minutes, he motioned me to crawl up. The ram looked better than good, but he was bedded in the open, certain to see us if we tried to get closer. All we could do was hunker down and wait, hoping they would give us a chance before dark. The last of our food and water was shared. What gear I had brought was divided up among the others, lightening my load.

The rams stood to feed and eventually worked their way out of sight. We gave them some time and then moved across an open area huddled and crouched together, stopping every few steps so Randy could glass. After losing some elevation he guessed we were safe. For the second time in the Yukon I chambered a round with purpose.

Randy edged ahead and soon found the sheep feeding down a chute below. He waved me forward and for the others to stay put. They didn't argue. I caught up then followed, first crouching then crawling then scooting until we could see the top of the big ram's back above some rocks. By the time he had cleared and showed his shoulder, I'd worked into something of a shooting position and squeezed the trigger.

My Kimber 8400 in .300 WSM is an honest, 1-inch rifle. The light was good and the ram was not that far. I'd used it to kill other animals at twice the distance. I don't think I was rattled, either. But he didn't drop at the shot. I really can't offer an excuse, but I hit him too far back. He stayed on his feet while I prodded another round into the chamber and started to squeeze.

Randy reached over, put his hand on my rifle and said, "He's going down now."

The ram fell and rolled down the mountain, deserving better. I was ashamed of myself when I lifted his head from the rocks.

A long day turned into a long night while we packed him over the mountain and to the cabin. Supper was waiting, and we ate big and fast and then headed for bed. The next day was spent in camp, caping and fleshing and napping. The propane-heated shower felt better than good and my boots got dry for the first time in a week.

We split up the next morning and hunted grizzly. In late summer the bears make looking for food a full-time job, so it wasn't unusual to find one moving across an open slope or working a creek. We had been seeing grizzlies almost every day, but none of the big ones were close enough for a shot. We were hunting for boars, almost always alone this time of year, and all the lone bears we glassed were far away and moving fast.

The other group noticed a bear across the main drainage not long after they left camp. He looked good, so the guide broke brush down the mountain then up the other side. I saw where they climbed for the bear and it made what we did for sheep look easy, but when they topped out in the basin where the bear had been, it was gone. Shedding packs, they flopped down in the grass with their lunches and soon saw their bear wading the creek far below, near where they were sitting when they first saw him. Down they went and soon found the bear coming their way but still out of range. They closed, but he was gone again when they looked around the last bend in the creek.

We spotted what was probably the same bear the next morning, several miles away and digging for marmots. We rode toward him, gaining most of the elevation on horseback. The last of the stalk was on foot, a steep climb up a trough scraped into the side of the mountain by a little trickle of water. At the top we found tracks, but no bear. Sheep were everywhere, and the view from the top was one of the highlights of my hunt. Near the little pass we came upon a huge moose skull, stark white against the contrasting green grass. Along with the sheds we kept finding along the creeks, it hinted that this area could be very interesting come late September.

Back at the top we spotted another bear. This one walked with a rolling swagger. He had a long neck, short legs and ears on the side of his head, all marking him as big. I really didn't have the climb in me, but I lied again because I wanted him so bad.

An hour later we tied the horses in the bottom and started up. The brush was terrible, so we worked our way along a narrow, thundering creek. Randy kept the dog ahead, hoping it would keep us from stepping on the bear if things didn't work out right. A large bowl was at the top, and when we parted branches at the bottom, the bear was going up the other side. He was too far. We might have caught him if he'd stopped to feed, but he didn't. Even then, he was moving around the mountain where the other guys were watching. We hoped they'd be looking at the right place when he broke cover and have time to do something about it, but they walked into camp before the saddles were off our horses. They never saw him.

The bears were there, but we didn't bring one back this time. Three weeks later things might have been different with moose. We glassed some mountain caribou, but didn't see the kind of bull that made us forget everything else, though some of the biggest heads taken lately have come from these mountains. None of that mattered one bit.

When we headed for the airstrip, two sets of golden horns were lashed on the packhorse I followed down the trail. Riding above everything else, the curls brushed against the branches, scattering bright yellow leaves into the creek that wound its way through the mountains and across moose flats to the Pelly. Somewhere ahead leading the string was one of the toughest men and finest guides I've ever followed up a mountain. Few are lucky enough to have such an adventure.

An abbreviated version was published in the September/October 2008 issue of Sporting Classics.

Jocelyn Russell
© 2009

Chapter 20

Waterbuck on the Side

More than anything else, we were there to hunt elephants. At least I was, and held what my mother refers to as "high hopes" about the whole thing. Sure, there would be opportunity for plains game with maybe a leopard or two thrown in, plus the real possibility of a lion if the permit came through in time. Intentions were to film it all, which does not make anything easier.

No matter, I had myself convinced, this year it would happen. My elephant luck would change.

Jamy Traut had turned in his usual super-human effort to coordinate every detail. Our past success with other game is why this would be our sixth hunt together in the northeastern corner of Namibia.

We'd planned a pretty ambitious safari for having just 12 days, and foremost among our goals was taking both of the elephant bulls that had been chasing cars, knocking down fences and raising general chaos on the Eden Conservancy.

I had something of a shirttail relationship with these bulls. Over the years I had watched and photographed them many times, seen the damage they had caused to all manner of property and listened to the stories of what the tellers believed were narrow escapes.

Jamy had secured permits that would allow us to take these two bulls as problem animals. I think we were both surprised when I turned down the opportunity to hunt one of them. More to the point, I had agreed to pass these permits along to friends in hopes that I could take a larger bull from Jamy's nearby concession in Bushmanland. This was a gamble on my part, given the time of year and the general long odds of taking a big elephant.

Four of us chartered a plane out of Windhoek, landed on the dirt strip at Eden, and soon we were taking turns at the bench verifying zero. Holes appeared in the targets right where we wanted, and we started hunting as soon as the last of our gear was loaded on the trucks.

The plan for our first day was simple: Everyone would go separate ways for plains game, while looking for any sign of the elephant herd that included the two bulls. Once the herd was found, every effort would be made to work either one or both designated hunters close enough for a shot.

The cloudy part was that the bulls needed to be far enough away from the herd so the shots would not draw a charge. There were a dozen or so baby elephants thereabouts, and Jamy was rightfully concerned that the cows would be very protective. Taking these two bulls was the priority of the hunt. My chance, if there was one, would come later.

Our short first day did not produce anything in the way of elephants, but everyone had the opportunity to take or turn down other animals. I didn't shoot, but I should have. As always, I had kudu on the brain, and when an exceptional springbok ram showed up, I waited and hesitated and made excuses until he finally faded away in the brush.

"He was something," I managed.

"He was more than that," came the reply.

The following morning someone spotted the elephant herd and the bulls were together, feeding some distance away. Straws were drawn, camera gear was checked and the hunters went after them, constantly playing the wind. The wind played right back, and after four hours of crawling through the thorns almost to the point of getting a shot, the group could only watch helplessly as the bulls rejoined the herd. Writing the morning off as good exercise, they kept the skinners busy with the game they took that afternoon.

While there is no way of knowing for certain what might be the shortest elephant hunt in recorded history, what happened the next day is a contender. One of Jamy's trackers found the herd late in the morning, and from a distance he watched the bulls feeding almost a mile away from the others. Even better, they were separated by one of the Kalahari's huge dunes. Good fortune continued, and they almost immediately found the truck of the designated hunter with all aboard, having just returned from an unsuccessful eland stalk.

Everyone grabbed their big rifles; the cameraman changed film and off they went, tacking into a dependable wind. In less than an hour Jamy had positioned them in the elephant's path and the larger of the two bulls rounded a tree at 12 yards.

Seeing the hunters standing in a small opening, the bull turned to come. A perfect frontal brain shot collapsed him in his tracks, and the back-up shot fired through the rising dust was unnecessary. Five hours later there was nothing left of the bull. All the people of Eden showed up to help butcher and every bite of meat was taken. Some steaks were cut from the cheeks and we had them the next night. They were wonderfully flavored and quite tender.

The following evening PH Wouter Hugo returned from his recon in Bushmanland. After washing the dust out of his throat, he announced that a big-footed leopard was hitting one of the baits. Moreover, the bait was finished, so another needed to be hung to give him something to chew on until someone could get out there and do what leopard hunters do.

I waited patiently for the elephant report while Wouter most carefully related details of world news heard over his radio, then casually offered that he had been spending the majority of his days watching an elephant that would "be to my liking." There is no good way to break bad news, but he made every effort.

"There is a difficulty. He's 13 kilometers outside the concession and moving the wrong direction. There is no water in this area to bring him back."

That said, a plan was made to keep track of the elephant while freshening the leopard bait as fast as possible. I took a zebra stallion for bait the next day, along with a big warthog in case the cat appreciated some variety in his meals. Wouter's truck headed out with a full load, with me fervently hoping that elephants sometimes change their mind, even if they never forget.

While I was collecting bait, Jamy found the second problem bull feeding far enough from the herd that a stalk was possible. This one turned out to be more difficult than the first, but they managed to work within 6 yards and took the shot that presented.

It was a bad angle, but the following shot moments later hit the brain. Now experienced in elephant butchering, Eden's residents quickly went to work on the carcass and the last load of meat was driven away four hours later.

I took a kudu bull that evening, a heavy-horned warrior that gave the impression of being something wonderful. The African night was dropping, and he looked good moving through the thorns. He was a great bull but did not crowd 60 like I'd hoped.

There is a little valley at Eden that's very special to me. I don't know why, as other locations only a couple of miles away are just as good, but I like to spend as much time there as I can. When word had come back that the leopard was all over the new zebra bait, Jamy grabbed one of the successful elephant hunters and hurried out to sit with him that afternoon. Someone else needed to leave the hunt early and was hoping to track eland, so I elected to spend the day hunting the valley and keeping out of everyone's way.

After checking the twisting wind and setting up in a good spot, it did not take long to see game. A big herd of blue wildebeest moved chaotically past, and some eland ambled through from the other direction. Gemsbok always seemed to be there, and small groups came and went.

Kudu began to show. First a group of young bulls, then cows with their big calves and finally the older bulls. Enough of the rut remained that they would raise the mohawks of their patchy winter manes at each other in warning. A tight cluster of waterbuck cows came next, close enough to hear their footsteps. Worried they would spook and alert the kudu, we dared not move, at least until the waterbuck bull trailing along stepped through a small opening in the brush.

There are but a handful of times in the life of even the most fortunate hunter that a truly magnificent trophy presents itself, an animal so unquestionably grand that you are powerless to move, afraid the blink of an eye or the vibration of another heartbeat will frighten him back to your dreams. It has happened to me on the northern Colorado plains with an antelope, in Alberta with an unbelievable elk and once more with a kudu only a few miles from where this waterbuck had appeared in the thorns. Two of those times I never had a chance, and I lost the opportunity for the kudu when he switched places with another I mistakenly shot.

I suppose it was with exaggerated care that I brought up the rifle and shifted left for a better view of the huge waterbuck bull. After gaining shooting position, I felt a slight confidence, then turned the power ring up to 6x on one of Leupold's new VX-7 riflescopes. Every twig snapped into focus.

Tracking ahead, I discovered what first appeared to be unobstructed shooting lanes were actually latticed with small branches. My confidence quickly disappeared.

Mostly by the sunlight glancing from the tips of his horns, I followed their slow procession, hoping for an opportunity. They finally stopped in some shade, the bull still covered by brush.

It took a long time for him to begin moving through the cows. I tracked every step, and the rifle jumped when he cleared and showed a shoulder. I lost him in the dusty scramble but felt good about the shot, then waited a little while, mostly to calm down. He had not gone far, taken through both shoulders by the stout Trophy Bonded Bear Claw bullet.

We radioed in the recovery truck, took pictures and then found a steel tape somewhere. Both horns measured well over 32 inches, the bases nearly 10.

The leopard did not come back that afternoon, but it did two days later. The sun was less than an hour from setting when it appeared on the designated branch. A perfect shot made recovery easy, and the pictures of the cat laid over a termite mound turned out to be spectacular.

Wouter came back in for supplies with mostly bad news. The big elephant was still moving away from the concession boundary and a good leopard had visited one of the far baits, finished it and then disappeared. With just a handful of hunting days remaining, all we could do was tie up more bait and hope he returned.

We did just that, but things did not work out. The leopard must have found something to his liking, and my elephant kept wandering farther away. Insult to injury, the lion permits did not show up as promised, even though several of the big cats were causing problems on ranches near Etosha.

Jamy and the other hunters hit a wonderful streak of luck. First it was a grand old eland bull they tracked across the dunes and finally caught in a good spot. Then it was a very good kudu and an even better gemsbok. It took two tries, but they also brought in a perfectly huge springbok ram, one that measured even better than the estimates around the fire the night after he was missed. Somewhere along the way they also managed a pair of duikers, a huge giraffe and a warthog someone just had to have.

For my part, I stayed focused on kudu. While I never found the kind of bull I was after, I did see several bigger than the one I had taken early in the hunt.

More importantly, I slowed down long enough to take a good red hartebeest and a blue wildebeest for a long-promised rug. There was even an opportunity to shoot some birds, something the trackers and their families seemed to appreciate very much.

After being home less than three weeks, I received a call from one of the other hunters. He had come back to the States for a business meeting, then returned to Namibia to hunt with another PH based not far from Eden. The lion permits had come available, and he had the opportunity to get one. They quickly took advantage of the opportunity, calling in a big lion with a very nice mane. Such it is for those with good luck.

I'm heading back to Eden a little earlier this year, hoping the elephant bulls will be on the right side of the boundary and that maybe a lion permit will show up in time. Jamy has promised to string up the leopard baits like Christmas lights, but another friend will have first crack. If it does not work out for any of the big stuff, I'll hold out hope for a kudu with 5 feet of spiral. It matters little what happens. Nothing compares to simply being in Africa. 🐃

Originally published in the January/February 2009 issue of Safari *magazine.*

Jaclyn Russell
© 2009

Chapter 21

Shiras

My odds ran something like 40-to-1 against drawing the permit, so pulling it from the stack of mail was more than a surprise. I read it over several times to make sure my name was on it, then some more to verify it really was for moose. The permit was for the same western Montana area my wife, Kellie, had drawn the year before, and the two months we'd spent there until she took her bull gave me a great head start. Still, the season was just five weeks away, so the only logical thing to do was head out scouting. I was on the way as soon as I got my gear together.

I got home late that night. Kellie and the kids were already in bed, so after eating the dinner she had set out, I went to the gun cabinet and considered my options. The big Dakota seemed the best choice for moose. Firing a 200-grain Partition almost as flat and every bit as accurate as the target rifle resting in the next slot, it would certainly be up to the challenge. Then there was the Model 70, my first real rifle, given by a proud father and reluctant mother on my 14th Christmas. Almost as powerful as the Dakota, it was lighter and would serve me well. Moose was first among my father's unrealized hunting dreams, so maybe it would be a good way to take him along. Then there was the lever gun. It would certainly do the job, and open sights would force me to get close.

Finalizing my mental inventory, I reached for the key, already knowing the answer. I unlocked the lower drawer and drew out my Freedom Arms .454 Casull. Taking the gun and a hot cup of coffee outside, I sighted on a weathered fencepost in the moonlight while considering the kind of

169

moose I wanted. With such an opportunity, I resolved to devote the entire season looking for something special. In the process, I knew I would have to pass up lesser bulls, as well as elk and deer if the permit was still in my pocket when their seasons came around.

I learned long ago that the best way to prepare for a trophy hunt is to do some scouting by phone, and over the next weeks I spent every free moment talking with people from the game department, forest service and B.L.M., as well as friends who lived in the area. I kept coming up empty. Finally, on a call to a friend of a friend, I heard what I wanted. The voice on the other end belonged to an outfitter. Only two days before he had spotted a moose, the best he remembered seeing. While he admittedly knew little about judging moose, his description told me this was the one I needed to find. The old boy had been in the outfitter's favorite elk area for several years and was unusually light in color. The grizzled bull, as he called him, had more than once made him grab for his .44 Magnum when it exploded from willow thickets in front of his horse. I had a place to start.

I can't remember how many miles I walked scouting for that bull before opening day. I searched an area 10 miles across, but with few roads and many deep canyons, a hundred moose could have lived there unseen. I looked morning and night, spending the days fishing the beaver ponds with my young son, Ross, and napping with him in the warm autumn sun. Not once did we see another person. I kept in touch with the outfitter, but he had lost track of the bull, even though his hunters and guides were working the area every day. Frustrated, I decided to try locating the bull by calling, even though it was still early for the rut. That didn't work either.

Calling moose is almost the opposite of calling elk, and it's hard to believe the sounds these animals produce. Cows do most of the talking. A cow looking for a bull issues a low, nasally groan something like that of a milk cow. It can last almost half a minute, and the cows usually make their calls in pairs. Theoretically, any bull within hearing distance, which is considerable, will soon show up.

The males respond with a series of low, resonant grunts that are difficult to hear from very far away. Bulls have a reputation for bad tempers, and with their ability to pinpoint the spot where a call originated, it's wise to keep a close watch upwind after imitating a cow.

170

Before the hunt I used commercial calls, but quickly discovered more realistic sounds could be made without them. Cupping my hands and pinching my nose, I could mimic a cow quite well after a bit of practice. Grunting was even easier. I proved this theory by calling in a number of young bulls and cows before the season. Fresh rubs and muddy wallows surrounded by big tracks confirmed I was in the right place.

Winter is never far away in the Rockies, and nights were cold by the time the season opened in mid-September. I wanted to take the family along, but my children were too young to be comfortable in a tent. A call to friend Lee Tracy secured the loan of his guest cabin, and a morning fire in the barrel stove kept everyone cozy. Lee also had a thinly disguised desire for moose steaks, so an offer to share sealed the deal.

Long before daylight on opening morning I headed for a small lake that held the most promise. After driving to the top of an isolated mountain, I parked and then made my way down toward the water in full dark. Frost covered everything, and my breath hung in the still air like smoke from a pipe. The Casull felt good under my arm, and an extra layer of wool kept me warm.

Approaching the lake, I was surprised to hear bulls fighting, the sound of clashing antlers mixing with splashes and excited grunts. Shooting light was at least 20 minutes away, but I picked them up through binoculars as soon as I reached the shore. They were on the other side, two black forms wrestling several hundred yards away, with another standing nearby. I crept around the lake, moving through the trees when I could hear them sparring, stopping when they stopped. They would mind their own business for several minutes, then one would grunt and the shoving would resume. Between rounds they would go back to browsing on willows and whatever else was to their liking.

I came to a point jutting out into the lake and carefully pushed through the reeds. Soon the back of one moose and then the other animals appeared. They were just in range. Finding a log that would serve as a good rest, I caught my breath and gave my best impression of a cow followed with several bull grunts, then carefully pulled the pistol from its holster.

All three moose jerked their heads in my direction, and for the first time I could see that one was a cow and both of the bulls were young.

A third bull grunted from the trees, and following the sound, I caught a flash of antlers. He came out at 70 yards, and was much bigger than the others. Throwing up the pistol, I waited for a clear shot, sighting on an opening where I expected him to appear. All I saw were two huge palms turning, and he moved quickly back in the direction he'd come. My calls did nothing to turn him, and the others soon followed.

I spent the rest of the morning trying to run him down. He had disappeared into a deep canyon and never answered my calls. Returning to the lake, I watched through the evening. A cow came, then another with her calf, but nothing else.

Passing a gas station on the way back to the cabin, a call to the outfitter confirmed he'd come up empty. Ross was waiting up for me back at the cabin. He had caught his first fish that day, a nice wild trout from a nearby creek. It was hard to tell who was more proud, him or his mother.

The next two days were a repeat of opening day. Moose were everywhere at first and last light. Some came to my calls, but most simply appeared near a lake or beaver pond. The elk were in full rut as well, and I bumped into them constantly while stalking through the woods. On the way home the third night, I called the outfitter at the arranged time. Even before he told me, I knew by his excited greeting that he'd seen the big bull.

An hour later, over coffee at his cabin, he laid out the story. With two of his hunters, he had worked on a herd of elk all morning near a small pond at the top of the mountain close to where I'd been calling. On the way out they had surprised two moose, and one was his grizzled bull. Promising to let him know how it turned out, I headed back to join my family at the cabin.

I had fished a series of beaver ponds near the lake where he'd seen the bulls and remembered how to get there in the dark. It was a long hike, so I packed light, taking only what was necessary. When I got close, I slowed and carefully glassed each dark shape, all the while listening for calls. Just before first light, one of the shadows moved. Kneeling to get a better view, the binoculars picked up antlers twisting through a willow thicket. The bull, a young one, had no idea I was there.

Edging forward to close the distance, I knelt behind a big tree when

172

a cow called just yards away. As soon as her call died, a second bull grunted back from somewhere off to the side. Figuring the larger bull was probably with the cow, I turned my attention to him. In the coming light I soon located the cow. The bull with her grunted again, and began rubbing his antlers on a dead tree that wobbled against the coloring sky. I couldn't see him, but listened as he popped branches from the trunk. Training binoculars on the tree, I watched until he stepped clear and noticed his rack was much larger than that of the other bull.

An old mining access road that was mostly grown over ran toward the big bull. Now little more than a horse trail, it was still a good shooting lane. I wrestled with whether to call or wait it out, but the cow made my decision for me. She began working her way toward the small bull and soon crossed just ahead. The big bull didn't like that and tried to head her off. The noise he made working his antlers through the brush covered the metallic clicks of thumbing the hammer. I put the crosshairs of the 2x Leupold on the trail, then peered over the top, waiting for the bull to show himself. He stopped at the edge, his head still in the trees. Only then did the light play off his grizzled coat. This was the bull I was after, so I gave a soft grunt.

The bull spun toward the sound and started coming at a fast walk. The instant I had a clear shot, I fired. He stopped like he'd hit a wall, then turned to run back down the trail toward the ponds. I fired again as soon as he was broadside and he went down. The younger bull stood looking at the cow for a moment, then followed her into the swamp.

I returned for my Jeep, then drove as close as I could to the animal. After caping and quartering the bull, I managed to get the pieces loaded. That night Lee was more than happy to let me hang the quarters in his meat house. Ross helped until the job was finished. I insisted that Lee keep half of the meat and don't recall that he put up much of a fight.

They tell me my bull had the largest antlers of any Shiras' moose ever taken with a handgun. I'm not sure how I feel about that; I only know that hunting Montana moose through the last weeks of summer is something I want to do again. Twenty years have come and gone, and I'm still waiting for another permit that says I can. 🐂

Originally published in the Summer 1993 issue of Game Journal.

Jocelyn Russell
© 2009

Chapter 22

Prairie Deer

The opportunities to hunt whitetails are almost endless. Just about every hunter in America can chase our most popular big game animal after a short walk or drive from home. Mule deer are a little different, but even first-time nonresident hunters can find plenty of them on public lands throughout the West. Deer are everywhere. Big bucks are another story.

While honest-to-God trophy bucks can and occasionally do turn up anywhere, we all can recite the well-known hotspots like a part from a Sunday school play. For whitetails: Alberta, Illinois and Iowa. Giant mule deer come from Utah, Sonora and Arizona. Apologies if I didn't mention your favorite, but I'll tell you mine. The reason I like Colorado so much is that both huge whitetails and monster mule deer live there. A tag in your pocket means you can hunt either of them – not just on the same hunt or even the same day – but at the same time. Try to find another place like it and please let me know if you do. Until then, I am going back to this spot every chance I get.

I don't know why the Colorado state line was drawn where it was, but there must have been a reason. Maybe to put a stop to Colorado and get started on Kansas. Maybe two neighbors didn't get along. Maybe an unimaginative cartographer with a straight edge liked the looks of the black line heading south from Nebraska. Maybe it was politics, since the Republican River winds through this country. For certain, it wasn't topography, for everything is pretty much the same on both sides. Plains mixed with rolling hills and dry creekbottoms. Wheat fields and cattle fences and receding willow bottoms running together. Thickets of Russian olive, dirt roads and cornfields appearing in orderly rotation. Not all that many deer live there, but some of them are really special.

T om Tietz is an interesting fellow. He doesn't have what my father would call a real job, which suits him fine. Tom makes his living photographing wildlife and guiding hunters. Some of those hunters end up at a farmhouse on the eastern edge of Colorado with a deer tag in their pocket and a decision to make. Around the dinner table the night before the hunt, between his impressions of a pack-lipped, redneck cable TV hunting show host, Tom will ask each hunter what type of deer he wants. If you don't answer right away, he will tease you in character with an antler picked from a pile of fresh sheds that he can reach from his chair.

"Found this one 'crost the road in the bottom last week. Figured him for about one-sebn-tee-five, maybe more. Whadda you think, Bubba? Bet they don't raise no whitey-tailed deer like this where you come from!"

The part of his routine that isn't funny is that the shed really did come from across the road and really was picked up the week before. If that doesn't get you thinking, out come pictures of big deer and happy hunters. Everyone else at the table measures you while you make up your mind, and then it's their turn to decide.

Ron Spomer, the Rifles Columnist for *Sporting Classics* and I were there to look for big deer. While I really wanted a whitetail, my mind was open. The idea going in was that I would hunt whatever Ron didn't. He finally decided on mule deer. That suited me just fine, because the night before Tom had driven through a fresh-cut cornfield not a mile from where we were sitting. His headlights first hit a family of raccoons, then a skunk, then a group of whitetails. One stopped his heart.

Another client hunting with Tom knew big deer, too, and the buck stood still for them a long time. Through binoculars they could estimate its size. They agreed that two tines on each side were at least 16 inches, maybe more. He was like a picket fence all the way out, and thick.

"I have a buck spotted that will crack one-sixty and another over one-seventy near a ladder stand two miles down the river. This one is far bigger," Tom said.

I shouldn't have asked how big they thought this deer looked to them, but I did. They answered me at the same time and with the same number. I was hooked.

Prairie Deer

Long before light the next morning we dropped off Ron to glass for a mule deer the landowner had seen, then carefully set up on the ledge of the cornfield where the big whitetail had been feeding. The moon was full, and it was hot and dry. The leaves were crunchy and ankle deep. The rut was two weeks away. Everything was against us. Between flocks of wild turkey, several bucks appeared, including one that I would have shot just about anywhere else. The one we wanted didn't show.

The weather was also holding the mule deer tight, so we got together late that morning and decided to still-hunt the canyons just across the river from the cornfield. Tom thought the big buck might be lying up there instead of along the river where the cows were so bothersome. It was shirtsleeve and sunscreen weather by then, but we gave it a try.

It pains me to tell it, but we made a two-hour hike to the top of a canyon and back, peering into every nook and finding nothing but does and coyotes. Returning to the truck, I excused myself to walk over the hill and find a bush. Shortly, I heard a shot. Just one, and I figured coyote. Then I remembered Ron didn't have a license for coyotes, which Colorado requires for some unknown reason.

I hurried back to the truck. Everyone looked pale and wide-eyed and tried to shout their version of the story at the same time. A big whitetail had come out running at less than 200 yards. Their rifles were unloaded and in the truck, and everything happened the wrong way before it got worse. By the time Ron had his gun and ammo sorted out, the buck was cresting a hill and had almost doubled the distance. A tagged-out hunter was still standing in the truck bed where he had been shouting instructions and scores and tine length and generally willing the shot to be taken because he had "Never seen a buck that big alive!"

Tom was shaking his head, having aged ten years while waiting for a shot while Ron wrestled his barrel away from a barbed wire fence. He got it clear just as the buck hit the top of the hill and missed him clean. I would have missed too, given all that encouragement and the strong crosswind.

I wanted to know if it was the buck we were after. Tom said, "Nope."

Then I asked, "How big??"

Still in the truck bed and reaching for something in the ice chest, the other hunter said simply, "He looked book."

We ate a quiet lunch then hit it again. Both Ron and I saw good deer. Back at the cornfield, I ran out of daylight before anything of interest joined dozens of other deer feeding around the edges. A big mule deer almost got shot a few miles away, but Ron thought he was a little light on the left front fork. Not far from the ranch a beautiful whitetail danced through the headlights and gave me something to dream about that night.

The weather didn't improve, so the next morning I climbed into the ladder stand after filling a nearby scent dripper. At least it would be quiet up there. Light came and so did the deer. I rattled and grunted. Does and little bucks snuck and trotted and stalked through the olives. Little bucks were chasing does and the bigger bucks were chasing little bucks. One of them came in and stood like a pointing dog at 40 yards almost daring me to shoot, both of his thick white antlers snapped off close to his head. A good-looking buck moved slowly through the thick stuff and finally stuck his head in the open. I was on him and ready, but a broken tine saved him. Even then, he would have been my best whitetail.

Other hunters reported broken-antlered deer. Maybe the rut was beginning and fighting was the reason, but Tom thought the extraordinary drought might have caused the antlers to be brittle. I think he was on to something, because almost every buck brought in that week was broken.

Tom and I spent the second afternoon back in the riverbottom near the ranch house looking for the big buck and fighting the swirling wind. It was so hot that we didn't need coats until sundown. Deer were everywhere, but not the one I was after.

The next morning it was back to the ladder. After a few hours Tom and Ron came to pick me up. Nothing interesting had moved, but a cowboy had told Tom about a big buck he'd watched bed down just up the creek the day before. We decided to make a drive to see if he was still in the area. I sure wish we'd gone straight to the truck.

The thick stuff I'd been watching all morning bordered a field of winter wheat. Tom and I walked along a fence at the field's edge, trying to be quiet and to keep from sinking into the mud from the latest pass of the big pivot sprinkler. Ron bird-dogged through the thick stuff below. We hadn't gone very far when several deer blew up underfoot.

I spun the rifle off my shoulder, turning to watch as they raced through the brush toward the trail we'd walked down just moments before. They were all does but I was shot through with adrenaline, so when Tom started yelling my name and I turned to see a buck clearing the fence and low-running across the field, I fell apart.

In his defense, Tom didn't actually tell me to shoot. Still, the urgency and volume in his voice, combined with all those white points sticking up over the buck's head convinced me he'd gotten a good look and that it was a keeper. It was a great shot, but I wish I'd missed. A nice 5x5 that goes about 140, he was two or three years too young to reach his potential. Several of the bucks I'd already passed were better, to say nothing of what we knew was there and hiding. Such is my luck with whitetails.

That afternoon we got everything right. Tom leases several ranches in the area, and we drove to one in hopes of getting a good look at a tall mule deer Ron had spotted earlier that morning. We found him, and through the Swarovski spotting scope carefully looked him over. He had it all. Almost. So we left him with a couple of cute does and headed toward a vantage point where we could set up and glass a fresh-cut cornfield.

Ron Spomer is one of those hunters who always seems to be in the right place at the right time. He recently hunted white sheep in Alaska with an outfitter known far and wide for taking rams around 36 inches and killed one that went 44 the first morning. We hunted elk in the same Idaho canyon several years ago with different outfitters. I heard one wimpy bugle in seven days while suffering through the worst hunt imaginable. He took a fantastic 6x6 and lived like a king for a week.

So when I looked out the side window and saw a big mule deer buck with points going every direction, it really wasn't much of a surprise. Of course, we had just crossed onto one of Tom's leases.

We drove out of sight and then stalked back to the buck. The does blew out of the canyon, but he stopped to look back like his kind has for generations. Ron's rifle barked and soon we were admiring a thick set of dark antlers running 27 wide with six points on one side and nine on the other. A great buck. Anytime, anywhere.

Originally published in the 2003 Deer & Big Game Rifles Annual.

Jocelyn Russell
© 2009

Chapter 23

Spiral Horns &
Man-Eating Crickets

Chances are good that anyone who has picked up a rifle and then tracked or climbed or sat somewhere waiting for something wild to walk by has entertained at least a flittering thought of becoming a professional hunter. Not the North American version, but African, the real deal.

Imagining yourself as an outfitter just does not hold the same attraction as being a "PH," and while neither career carves a path to wealth, it's pretty certain the PH will have better luck with girls. After all, it's hard to stand stories of deer or elk or even a grizzly up against something from the big five. Double rifles impress. Cobras trump rattlesnakes. A khaki safari jacket with its row of big cartridge loops beats all to hell blue jeans with a chew-can ring worn into the back pocket.

A few dream so hard and long that they do something about it, heading to Africa with hopes of finding work in hunting camps as skinners or drivers. Those showing promise eventually get invited to follow the hunting procession after rounds are chambered.

Over time they work forward in the line of march until the PH moves their tassel left by asking how best to approach an especially large elephant in thick cover or where the biggest sable he's ever seen might have gone after it took their scent.

Acceptance of this advice means next season they will get their own hunters to keep out of trouble. Those failing to impress either return home to find honest work or buy a movie camera, shoot buffalo in the gut so they can charge and sell tapes to people who should know better than to buy them.

Jamy Traut resembles Harry Selby from the early 1950s when he was dragging Robert Ruark and his typewriter across Africa. Growing up in Namibia on the property where he now hunts and keeps a home for his young family, Jamy came to live the dream honestly.

Someone named the place that Jamy hunts "Eden" in a moment of divine clarity because it really is – 70,000 private acres of brush and dunes and fields and riverbottoms filled with game.

Only one group at a time visits Eden, and Jamy treats them like they own the place. Hunters make the short trip from Windhoek, then spend however many days they can pry away from work and other pastimes that don't really matter looking for things like kudu, gemsbok and eland.

A few who speak up in advance get to include sable, leopards and maybe cheetah if one happens to be passing through. Another dozen or so plains game species can be added to the menu. So can the odd black rhino, but one of those commands enough real dollars that anyone back home holding sway over the checkbook needs a strong sense of humor. Further encouragement with roses and something that sparkles should be figured into that cost, especially if the grand plan calls for locating the full mount anywhere in her house.

Although Eden is managed for wildlife, it's far from a commercial operation. Jamy hosts a very limited number of hunters each season, certainly fewer than would like to come. He also carefully limits the amount of game taken so trophy quality is exceptional. More to the point, it isn't unusual to see 20 kudu bulls a day, but hunters kill fewer than that each year. Almost all these bulls stretch well into the 50s and a few carry 5 feet of horn around the curl.

While one of the most productive ways to hunt Eden is sitting in a blind downwind from a waterhole in the afternoon, hunters usually start the morning in the back of an open Toyota Hi-Lux looking for game or promising tracks. When you see something you like, off you go. Sometimes it works, sometimes it doesn't. You just keep trying, falling more in love with Africa each time you walk away from the truck. Give Jamy the choice and he will take you eland hunting. That means walking, because eland almost always come to water after dark. More than anything he loves to take a hunter and follow the tracks left by groups of old, tufted bulls. Sometimes it takes several days to get a shot. It could also happen in an hour.

Our party of four flew to Windhoek, sailed through customs and met Jamy as he herded a train of luggage carts in our direction. Two of us had been there before and knew the routine, so things went quickly.

Once outside we filled a waiting truck with gear, then climbed into a chartered plane. An hour later we landed on a wide gravel road near the main camp, fired a few rounds to make sure our rifles were still pointing in the right direction and started hunting. Simple as that. Everything we might need for the day was waiting in the trucks.

Jamy had brought in a second PH to help and he could not have made a better choice. Danny Bartlett is gentle giant of a man. He knew his way around Eden and could determine the trophy quality of an animal almost instantly. A professional hunter much of his life – and with the stories to back it up – he was an absolute pleasure in the field as well as around the fire each night.

Pairing off for the day, I partnered with an old friend who had brought me to Africa several years before on the first safari for both of us. He now willingly accepts credit for ruining both of our lives in the doing. We argued like old women over who would get first shot and finally tossed a coin with a kudu on one side that we figured for "heads." He lost, but I gave him the first shot anyway because I did not want to rush any part of Africa.

That business concluded, we climbed into the open-backed hunting truck and pressed rifles into empty racks. Jamy passed out apples and we ate them while sorting gear as the truck moved down the main road.

An African version of rush hour traffic played out, with stop-and-go animals everywhere, and we had to look at every single one of them with first-day enthusiasm. A herd of impala with two good rams appeared around the first corner. The rams shoved each other until one of them proved whatever it was that needed proving, then they walked off together as if all was forgiven.

Two kudu bulls crossed ahead, backward-pointing horn tips

betraying a tender age. Gemsbok and zebra and both flavors of wildebeest stood in the distance and never broke rank as long as the truck kept moving. Warthogs prompted the telling of all the fart jokes learned from our kids.

We stopped the truck and walked quietly into a place where a mutual friend had taken a wonderful flared-horn kudu a year-to-the-day before. Once there, we watched a very good waterbuck come in for a drink.

"Almost there," said Jamy, "but we have eight days. Either of you taken one better?"

Any way you look at it, the answer was no, because neither of us had taken a waterbuck, let alone one better, so we trusted Jamy but walked away shot through with remorse.

On the way back to the truck we crossed a high point and heard a shot in the distance. Actually, everyone else heard it. With a checkered past of loud rock and roll music and short-barreled Model 29s, I just took their word for it. We beat the other truck to camp and they pulled in proud with two zebra stallions and one great warthog to show for their efforts.

The warthog hunter had kids, too, so we told our fart jokes again and he added several of his own. Dinner was waiting and so was the rest of our gear in the sleeping tents. It didn't take long to turn in, everyone still knocked back by jet lag.

If by slim chance anything in a hunter's life can compare to watching an African sunrise, then I surely cannot wait for it to happen to me. Standing around a fire until the horizon hints of pink, you brace against the morning's chill with hot coffee. Someone starts the trucks and after engines rattle themselves warm, you climb into the hunters' seats and wipe away the heavy dew so it won't soak through. It doesn't seem cold until the truck moves, then the wind hits your face and tears slide down your cheeks and spread into dark half-circles on your collar.

The guinea fowl and francolin are already out, swarming the roads. Hornbills squawk with contempt if disturbed from their perch. Herds of impala and springbok stand hunched against the cold and let the truck pass, not caring to move just yet. Then you see something or the tracks of something you came halfway around the world to hunt and just plain forget about the cold and the waiting thorns and the money it took to get there. You shrug away everything else, turn the bolt down over a round and fall in behind the PH and his tracker.

Often the track ends without a shot being fired. It gets covered by other tracks, the wind betrays or the animal at the end just isn't the one. Then there are times when everything goes amazingly right. That first full morning was one of those times.

Danny spotted several gemsbok in the distance and all agreed that one of them was something special. They moved in and Leupold's Mike Slack made an outstanding shot. Soon they were shaking hands over an outstanding gemsbok bull that went 41 inches.

Later that morning Danny worked along a dry river channel and Mike's partner took an exceptional waterbuck.

It went on like that for several days: a huge springbok ram then a big waterbuck for Mike, zebras and wildebeests and impala all around. Then we all got serious about kudu. The first big one was missed fair and square, and our stalks just didn't work. It had reached the breaking point when the giant cricket showed up.

Mike and his friend were sitting in a brushed-up ground blind looking at a waterhole surrounded by fresh kudu tracks. After settling in, someone noticed what looked to be the world's largest cricket. Thinking no one back home would ever believe a cricket could grow to the size of a chipmunk, someone dug in their bag and fumbled for a camera. At the click of the shutter they all heard a snort. It came from behind so they knew it wasn't the cricket. Everyone reached for a rifle and stood to see a seriously big kudu bull running away through the brush. It never was clear if a shot was fired, but everyone had a good laugh about it that night.

Two days later I ended up with Jamy in the cricket blind by accident. We were ahead of schedule and decided to wait there a bit before moving to another place with hopes of driving game to my partner in the process.

The blind was unusually small, and brush came up and somewhat over the top on one side. Only the hunter could see the shooting lane and everyone else was pretty much destined to sit low and hope for the best, or maybe take a nap. Any shot was close, owing to the small size of the clearing.

I threaded my Kimber Model 8400 .300 WSM through an opening in the brush, its butt held in place against my shoulder by shooting sticks. Resting binoculars over the scope, it was possible to watch the waterhole and take a shot without moving anything but one hand.

It didn't take long for kudu to come. First cows and young bulls, then good bulls faded in and out of sight in the brush. A herd of springbok came as well, a great ram running the show. I decided to take him if he was still there when we were ready to leave, but continued to watch the kudu. Soon, seven mature bulls were working the clearing. The rut was over but still fresh in their mind, so one or two at a time would step from cover to bump the drinking cows, just to make sure.

The old, gray bull came from behind the blind, so close he was out of focus when he appeared in my binoculars. He walked past the springbok ram and around to the other side of the water, where other bulls gave way. Even though he couldn't help me now, Jamy had described what a bull with a deep curl might look like, and this one was surely that.

I waited until he turned broadside and shot him at the point of the shoulder, making sure nothing else was behind to catch the Barnes XLC after it exited. Whipping the bolt, I watched the downed bull through the scope while three-dozen springbok and kudu tore away into the bush. Seconds later I heard snorting and caught sight of the springbok ram standing 30 yards away. I stood and shot him as he turned to run.

The kudu, far and away my best, went 58 inches around the curl. At more than 15 inches, the springbok also stretched well into the record book.

A day later I doubled again, first on a warthog with altogether too much teeth and then a long-horned waterbuck. Several miles away Jamy and his hunters took a brace of great kudu bulls after a long stalk.

Hunting at Eden is a wonderful experience, and Jamy is now expanding to include some of the best concessions in the Caprivi Strip and surrounding areas. He will be offering elephant, lion, leopard and buffalo. These hunts are filling as fast as details become available, especially after word got around that an elephant with a single tusk weighing 115 pounds was just taken and that the hair on the biggest lions looks like something from an '80s rock band. I'm already booked to go back three more times. Jamy and Eden are that good.

Originally published in the January/February issue of Safari *magazine.*

Jocelyn Russell
© 2009

Chapter 24

Kiwi Reds

Being a pretty serious elk hunter, I had always wanted to hunt red stag. The idea of stalking those roaring, crowned giants was wonderfully appealing, but never quite made it to the top of my wish list. Alaska kept calling me back, and there was a real need to make some tracks in Africa.

Almost by accident, I booked a hunt for red stag that would also include sika and fallow deer. It turned out to be one of the most exciting hunts I've ever experienced.

A call to booking agent Jack Atcheson Jr. about something else brought the suggestion of a free-range hunt in New Zealand for the first ten days of March. After working out the details, I convinced an old bird-hunting friend that he needed to come along, and soon we were flying over the Pacific.

Adrian Moody met us at the tiny Taupo airport. A professional meat hunter for much of his life, Adrian enjoyed hunting so much that he became a full-time outfitter and started Mountain Hunters Outfitting. While he guides on some of New Zealand's best game ranches, his specialty is free-range hunting. His professionalism and good nature have allowed him to secure exclusive hunting leases on some of the finest private property on the North Island.

We collected our gear and then made a quick stop at Adrian's home to pick up food and meet my guide. Gerald Fluerty is also a professional meat hunter, but this was to be his first trip as a guide. Like Adrian, he was polite, courteous, friendly to a fault and an expert in the mountains. A natural guide in every respect.

After four hours of winding roads, hunting stories and critical discussions about today's music, we unpacked into a clean cabin, what they call a hut, in the middle of an 80,000-acre sheep station. Adrian and Gerald had just completed a remodel, the best part of which was a shower with solar-heated hot water.

It didn't take much prompting to get started the next morning. Daylight slowly came as Gerald led the way upward through an impossibly green canopy of trees and bushes on the steep mountain above the cabin. The country varied almost beyond description. A look in one direction brought memories of hunting the sage and juniper flats near Flagstaff, Arizona. A turn of the head and the huge, dark canyons of Washington's Blue Mountains came to mind. Across the valley were the ridges and parks and meandering creeks of Montana's Yellowstone country. Far away stood the sheep mountains of the Yukon.

Familiar smells and bird calls from those places mixed with others that were strange and exciting. Pineapple trees stood in the shadow of ponderosa pines. Hedgehogs tiptoed across the trail. Untold thousands of sheep milled about in pastures across the valley, looking for all the world like a frothing river during runoff.

We topped the mountain and circled through a sheep pasture to gain the wind before approaching an overlook above a deep basin. Several days earlier Adrian had spotted a group of red stags feeding down its steep walls. One of them was exceptional. Since the rut was still weeks away, he hoped they would still be nearby.

The first stag I'd ever seen stepped into the sun far below, about the same time Gerald was anchoring the spotting scope on its tripod. Gerald looked it over through binoculars while I red-lined the power ring of the 60x Swarovski. Another soon joined him. Both were young stags, with classic red-shaded coats that contrasted vividly with their wiry, gray muzzles. We watched as they fed through small openings. Two more worked into the top of the basin on

190

separate trails and a third joined them from a hiding place. None of the newcomers was big enough to stalk, but one would likely be a first-day shooter next year.

After the stags disappeared, we alternately glassed across a huge valley while keeping an eye on the basin below. We didn't locate the big stag, but did see plenty of sika deer too far away to judge. Gerald whispered that this ranch was regarded as the finest free-range sika property in New Zealand and that we should be very patient and selective. Given the amount of game visible that first hot morning, it would have been hard to argue that point.

Back at camp for lunch, Adrian reported seeing more than 100 head of red and sika deer, including three grand sika stags.

Soon Gerald and I were climbing again, this time to an area closer to where we'd glassed all the sika deer that morning. By the time the sun was setting we quit trying to count the animals feeding through the lush parks far below.

Just before dark a pair of sika stags appeared, chasing younger stags and hinds across an elevated bench. Gerald looked them over through binoculars and pronounced them worthy of a stalk the following morning. Farther up the mountain another stag appeared. Even in the failing light, he appeared to be larger than the other two.

The next morning we climbed for the three big sika stags while Adrian hunted another part of the ranch. The climb took longer than expected and we spent much of the day hiding from rain under a rock outcropping above a valley full of red deer. Each time the sun came out so did more deer. We were all but surrounded by herds, but none of the stags was what Gerald would call a "boomer." Waiting until evening, we began a long stalk down the mountain for the sika stags from the night before.

A series of sloping, grassy meadows meandered down the mountain. Some were only dozens of yards across while others covered several acres. Each was surrounded by a wall of brush and trees. Enough rain had fallen to deaden any sound and a light wind was running uphill.

The first two clearings were empty. The pitch of the mountain became steep as we worked our way down, forcing us to walk carefully on the slick grass. The third clearing came into view. Moving around a juniper to get a better view of the edges, I slipped. As I fell into a sitting position, I caught a movement. A big sika stag had stepped into the clearing below and lowered his head to feed. His antlers seemed as tall as his body.

He didn't know we were there and moved farther into the open. Gerald quickly sized him up and whispered that he was the one we were after. While he got his videocamera going, I took a wrap on the sling and dug in my heels. The stag dropped at the shot.

The sika was easily one of the most beautiful big game animals I'd ever seen. Caught up in admiring him, it took a long time to realize my guide was even more excited than I was. Gerald thought him to be exceptional, a massive 4x4 with heavily beaded main beams.

It was a long walk back to camp. Adrian came as far as he could in an ATV to meet us, and we were greeted with a telling smirk. A huge sika, virtually a bookend to mine, was hanging behind the hut. Stories went long into the night.

Having failed to find the big red stag, Adrian suggested moving camp to another sheep station the next day. The manager there had seen a good stag recently, so it didn't take much convincing. Soon we were climbing another mountain and once again glassing reds as they fed out of the thick cover. Back at the truck we compared notes and drew up a plan for the next day. Adrian had spotted a big stag just at dark. While too far away to judge, he appeared to have it all.

According to the plan, we would split up and work different sides of likely bedding cover. Hopefully, one of us would catch the stag out in the open. It might have worked, except there were so many animals we were unable to walk more than a few minutes without spooking something. The morning a bust, we decided to set up over the area where he'd appeared the night before.

Gerald and I worked our way over the top of a hill above a game trail where we had watched the most traffic. Crawling the last bit, we encountered a bedded hind only 15 yards away. There was nothing to do but lay in the grass until she moved.

As the sun set, more deer appeared on the trail and kept us pinned. Then we heard a stag raking trees far below. Hoping it was the big stag and that he would come our way in time, we stayed in position.

The bedded hind stood and began to feed. While she hadn't spotted us, she was so close we couldn't move the last little bit to where we would be able to see the stag emerge from the trees.

With only minutes of shooting light left, we got a break. A family of brushy tailed opossums scampered down the trail, distracting the hind. As she moved off we crawled quickly forward, getting into position just as the stag stepped into the open.

Shadowed as he was, it was impossible to tell anything about his antlers, other than the length of the main beam. Gerald couldn't help this time; the decision was mine alone. Centering the reticle on the point of his shoulder, I touched the trigger. The *whock* of the bullet came back and the stag fell in his tracks.

When we got to the stag, I was disappointed to discover he was a young animal. While his main beams were long, he didn't have the antler mass or number of points of the classic red stag trophy. That's hunting. Sometimes you take a chance and everything works out the way you would like. Other times you want to call back the bullet.

Adrian was frustrated that we couldn't locate a big stag on this station and wanted to move again. We dropped off the meat and heads on our way through Taupo, then worked our way to another station that had both good reds and fallow deer. Agreeing that taking my partner's red took priority over everything else, we set out early that afternoon on a long climb.

Topping a mountain, four of us went to work with binoculars, and soon Adrian discovered a wonderful red bedded far away. The spotting scope showed him to be at least 7x7, with long main beams that almost met at the tips. Strips of velvet hung from his white antlers.

It wasn't long before we spotted another great stag not far from the first. This one had extraordinary mass that ended in wildly crowned tops. Both had racks that you'd expect to find behind a high fence, beyond anything even the luckiest hunter could expect free-range.

We decided to race darkness and try a stalk on the 7x7, even though it meant descending a steep mountain, fording a river and climbing the other side in just over an hour. We started down, but Adrian soon spotted another red farther up the valley. Through the binoculars he dwarfed all the others.

Realizing there was no way to close the distance in the remaining light, we broke out the spotting scopes. Looking through the 60x made it clear this bull was something special. His long main beams carried mass to the tips and his tines stretched out and up like bayonets. Two more stags, each much larger than the one I'd shot, came out and browsed nearby. By comparison, the first bull seemed twice as big as the newcomers.

We watched until dark then backed out of the valley. Over dinner we talked about what to do the following morning. It seemed best to glass from the same location at first light, looking for the stag and then waiting until he bedded. At the same time we would try to pinpoint all the other red and fallow deer, then stalk through them until we got within shooting distance. There were dozens of wild goats and pigs in the area, compounding the problem.

At first light we were all relieved to find the big stag near the same spot. What we thought would be a relatively quick stalk took four hours because of the steep terrain and a dangerous river crossing. Finally, after reaching a predetermined vantage point, we found his antlers rising out of the grass about 300 yards away. It seemed like everything was working out, but it quickly fell to pieces. One of the other stags approached him, posturing. They chased each other around, working their way over a hill and out of sight, and later back again.

Several times that afternoon we caught a glimpse of the stag as he fed or visited his wallow. We never moved, thinking he would come closer. Finally, with darkness falling, Adrian decided to stalk him in his bed. I stayed and kept watch as the trio worked their way around some hinds and crept into position.

Not long after I heard a shot. Three smiling faces were admiring the stag when I arrived. A 9x7 with wonderful mass, he was the largest red stag taken by any of Adrian's hunters in his 11 years of guiding and certainly one of the finest trophies of any species any of us had ever seen in the wild.

Returning the next morning, we took two exceptional fallow bucks with back-to-back stalks and shots, a beautiful conclusion to a wonderful adventure. After putting off a red stag hunt for so long, I can't wait to do it again. If nothing else, it offers a good excuse to return to one of the world's most picturesque countries.

Originally published in the March/April 2003 issue of Bugle *magazine.*

Jocelyn Russell
© 2009

Chapter 25

Hunting Buffalo in Harlem

Montana's Harlem is one of those towns you can only find on a road map the size of a bed sheet, the kind they still give away in gas stations and drug stores in parts of the West. If you had one of those maps laid out on the hood of a truck, it's pretty easy to find Highway 2 running about 50 miles south and parallel to the Canadian border. Locals call it the High Line. About halfway between Shelby and Glasgow on Highway 2, and just east of where Montana hooks into Alberta and Saskatchewan, there is a little dot.

Look real close. That's Harlem.

I like Harlem. People you've never seen before say hello like you had them over for dinner last night because your kids are thinking about getting married. The tire shop won't take your money for fixing a flat because "It happens," and the waitress/owner/baker at the only cafe open for lunch is now the cook because, "Charlie has a terrible infection in his legs that hurts him something awful when he stands in front of the grill." I doubt if poor Charlie is a better cook. Four of us ate and drank our fill there for a twenty, tip included, two days running.

Harlem is more or less the northwest corner of the Fort Belknap Indian Reservation. Even by Montana standards the reservation is a big chunk of property, nearly a million acres. The land hasn't changed much since someone drew its rectangular boundary. Both the Gros Ventre and the Assiniboine tribes share claim to the land. They take good care of it, too, including the big game. Fort Belknap has a strong wildlife management program. I've been there several times and the hunting keeps getting better.

Born a Hunter

At Fort Belknap it's possible to take bison, up to four antelope, a whitetail or mule deer buck, to shoot a fantastic variety of wild upland birds and even to melt your barrel in a prairie dog town, all in the space of a week. Other than the small stuff, hunting permits are limited and the trophy quality is very good, especially for bison and antelope.

The reservation has about 600 bison that live on 13,000 acres of native habitat in the rolling prairie surrounding Snake Butte, a prominent landmark that's culturally important to the tribes. This herd is rapidly expanding, to the point that another 4,000 acres was just added to their pasture. Once you pass through the gates, there are no cross fences to remind you of the modern reality that bison cannot be allowed to wander. It's easy to step back in time and get lost in the experience.

I booked tribal member Reno Shambo to guide us in late September when the antelope would be rutting and the bison would have their new winter coats. I had hunted with Reno several times before and enjoyed spending time with him. He is a fine guide and wonderful companion. Born and raised on the reservation, he knew where to go to get the best hunting and shooting for his clients. He's quite a hunter, and when we rolled in he was still in a funk about missing a 400-inch elk with his bow the week before. To hear him tell it, the only branch on that side of the mountain reached up and grabbed his arrow as it flew toward the bull.

Our plan was to hunt antelope in the morning and evening, and bison during the middle of the day. Reno had been scouting for two days before our arrival, and we showed up early enough in the afternoon to give antelope a try. He pulled in at Fish & Game just as we were getting our licenses and we raced to a spot where he'd watched a big antelope buck that morning.

We moved and glassed until dark without turning up anything more than 14 inches, but from our vantage points we could look far to the west and pick out bison herds grazing on the side of Snake Butte. When the sun nudged the horizon, we knew we'd have our chance tomorrow.

After spending the early part of the next morning stalking a wonderful antelope that kept giving us the slip, we met up with Mike Fox, director of the Fort Belknap Fish and Game Department, and two other wardens at the main gate of the bison area to talk over our hunt. The first order

198

of business was to learn how to judge a bison for trophy quality.

Mike explained that once a bull reaches 4 years, he's difficult to tell from onc that's 10 or more, unless you've had the opportunity to be around the older bulls. A trained eye looks for broomed horns that curl back in at the top and carry good mass the entire length. Older bulls have a more pronounced hump when viewed from the side, and their heads are wider.

The rut had ended weeks ago, so the old bulls had probably left the main herds and were off by themselves in small bachelor groups. Finding the main herds was easy. Finding the big boys was much more difficult due to the broken country, much of it untouched by roads.

We decided to split up, with a hunter in each truck, then took off in different directions, agreeing to meet at a tall butte several miles away after looking around. We drove and carefully glassed different bands from a distance and finally found several large bulls grazing near the top of our landmark butte. As we cut the distance, two more huge bulls appeared far below the others, so we closed on them while working our way toward the meeting place.

The other hunters were already there, glassing five more bulls working away from them in a little flat. We all agreed that at least two of them were bigger than any we'd seen. A coin toss had already decided who would be first up, so a Kimber .338 Winchester Magnum was pulled from the case and Mike Fox led the way.

I trailed behind, taking pictures of the stalk, and soon we were about 40 yards from the biggest bull. It took a long time for him to clear the rest of the group, then a 225-grain Barnes X caught him low in the ribs. Another followed with little effect, but a third in the shoulder brought down what surely was the grandest bull on the reservation.

We crowded a remaining bull away with the trucks, then returned to marvel at the mountain of animal lying on the prairie. Even Mike was amazed. The horns were broomed almost to the size of a tennis ball and even then were almost 17 inches long. The head was heavily scarred and massive beyond description. Examining the bull's teeth, Mike thought him to be about 13 years old and his weight just under a ton. The hoist on the meat truck broke when it tried to lift him.

It wasn't time to go after antelope, so we left the butchering crew and worked our way back toward the two bulls we'd spotted earlier. Now that we had some reference, we realized one of them was a grand trophy. We followed when they disappeared over a rocky hill, watching the wind and watching for rattlesnakes, until we caught them and set up in a good position.

Remembering how the first bull reacted at the shot, we decided to take this one higher. When the rifle roared, the bull bucked like he was slapped with a hot iron and ran in a wide circle. As soon as he stopped another shot pierced his lungs, but he stayed on his feet. He tried to charge the rifle, but a third shot drove him to the ground. The other bull moved away as we approached.

This bull was quite different than the first. Instead of being broomed and scarred, his wonderful horns were dark and shiny, sweeping out and back. The tips were perfect. Mike judged him to be about 12 years old.

We helped with the butchering, something that made us all appreciate the work of the old buffalo skinners who had no doubt labored in this same spot some 140 years before.

Now it was time for antelope and it didn't take long to find a big one. Reno spotted him trailing a group of does almost a mile away. He led the stalk several times while two of us remained on a vantage point to keep track of the herd. They worked him for hours and finally, just before the sun slipped behind the horizon, they were able to get in front of the herd as it ran in a wide circle. The buck showed and the shot was good. We arrived to find Reno dressing out a massive 16-inch buck with deep prongs – the best buck his hunters had taken that season.

The next morning we found a wonderful buck with wide, flaring horns and prongs that seemed to go on forever. He was in a flat several miles across with a hundred other antelope clustered in bands of a dozen or more. A mature buck commanded each band and tried to keep the does together. Smaller bucks worked the edges, hoping to pick off a doe when the boss wasn't looking. Since the ground was too flat for a stalk, we set up to push the big buck into some small ridges where a shooter was waiting. It was a great plan that almost worked. The buck doubled back and ran by on the wrong side, leaving no chance for a shot. He ended up back on the big flat where we left him.

We met up with Mike Fox and the crew at Snake Butte the next afternoon to go after my bison, then fanned out looking at the bachelor groups. I rode with Mike, and we bounced our way to the top of the butte to look over four bulls we'd seen from below the day before. We found them in some tough, wrinkled country, and then played a game of tag for the better part of an hour trying to judge their horns. They finally worked their way out onto a flat where I could see that two of them were larger than any of the bulls we'd seen that day.

I chambered a round and worked my way through the rocks to close the distance. As I did, one of the two big bulls came toward me. He was clearly the boss, and didn't like me crowding his group. I took a good rest over the rock and glassed back and forth between him and the other large bull, trying to determine which was better. The horns were similar in mass and length, but the closer bull had a larger head and more impressive cape. As he turned broadside I took him high, just behind the shoulder.

Back at the cafe, we decided to dedicate the balance of the day to the antelope with wide-flaring horns. We found him, and missed him. Then we found him again . . . and missed him some more.

A good buck made the mistake of coming over a hill where I was waiting in ambush, and Reno soon measured his heavy horns at just under 14 inches. At sunset another antelope dropped to a wonderful shot. We were done and happy, the wide buck was still out there somewhere, and we lingered on the prairie to watch one of the most spectacular sunsets any of us could remember.

The last morning we set out with borrowed shotguns through the creekbeds and CRP edges after pheasant, Huns and sharptails. It seemed birds were flushing with every step. In three hours we shot up every shell we could find and had enough birds to make a family of six a meal to remember. It was clear to all that Fort Belknap was a bird-hunter's paradise. Going back with a good dog and a fine, light double is high on my list.

At mid-morning we swapped the shotguns for .22 rifles and headed to the nearest prairie dog town. In fall, the little animals usually disappear as soon as a truck rolls over the horizon, but this time they were out. The wind picked up and made shooting difficult, but we still managed a good showing. We stayed long after we were supposed to leave, spotting for each other and laughing at the missed shots. It was a perfect way to end one of the most enjoyable hunts I've ever experienced.

Originally published in the May/June 2001 issue of Safari *magazine.*

Jocelyn Russell
© 2009

Chapter 26

Horns in the Driveway

The drive from my home to the Brown's family farm outside Torrington, Alberta, took all of a long day, but I had left early enough to enjoy some of the most spectacular scenery in North America. It also gave me plenty of time to think about elk. In the preceding six months I had fussed with the tune of a .300 Weatherby Magnum, assembled a duffel of polar hunting gear and generally worked my way into a frenzy of anticipation. Every time I thought of climbing Heartbreak Hill, where Clarence Brown had taken an elk many considered the finest North American trophy tagged in the last 50 years, I got chills.

This was my first guided hunt, so the predictable questions kept running through my mind. Would I miss a shot at a Boone & Crockett bull? Would an unseen stick popping underfoot ruin an otherwise perfect stalk? What if I fell off my horse?

I spent more time than I liked to admit telling myself it would work out for the best, trying to increase my confidence. I had fired better than 500 rounds through the rifle and knew it could do the job. I had killed elk with it at long range. I had researched equipment to the point I knew everything I had was either right or as good as I could afford, but nothing I ever thought of doing could have prepared me for the sight that greeted me in the Brown's driveway.

Actually, I wasn't sure I was in the right place until my headlights hit a fine 6x6 rack and then an enormous 7x7, both resting on a pile of pushed snow. They were fresh kills.

A lady who immediately introduced herself as "Barb Brown, Allan's wife" happened to be outside. She gave me the warm, genuine smile I would soon see from the entire family and told me supper was waiting.

"Come in and wash up. The house is a lot warmer than it is out here," she said.

I followed her in, trying not appear too excited over the bulls that seemed as tall as my Jeep. Supper, and I mean supper, was on the table in excess. My questions were asked and answered with equal enthusiasm. Between my curiosity of how hunting had been so far, theirs about my season back home and the drive in general, we had a full evening. Clarence's older son, Dale, even broke out a photo album filled with pictures of more trophy-class bulls than I imagined ever lived. I went to bed that night pinching myself to make sure the day I had looked forward to for so long was finally here.

We could not go to base camp the following day as the hunters already there had extended their stay, so I spent the morning getting in the way of Clarence and his younger son, Ron, while they did their chores. This extra day allowed me to do something I now hold more fondly than any other memory of the trip: I was able to get to know the Browns as a family and came to realize that each is as important to the outfitting business as the other.

Barb and Esther, Clarence's wife, keep the camp stocked with supplies, pack countless lunches and take care of hunters as they come in and out of the mountains. Grandma Brown, who has to be one of the most keen-witted and enjoyable people on the face of the Earth, provided all with a helping hand and moral support, as well as a contagious smile. Dale and Ron help out in camp as needed, and they're quite knowledgeable about elk and elk hunting. Ron, in fact, had killed the larger of the two bulls outside.

We headed west early the next morning, climbing into the Canadian Rockies. The Brown's camp is on the Panther River a few miles east of Banff National Park, and the area had been closed to vehicles for the first time in years. Instead of driving to camp as they had in the past, supplies were brought in on a big, wheeled wagon pulled by a team of draft horses. Guides and dudes rode in and out on horseback as well. Just a bit more than a week of the season remained, and other outfitters along the Panther had already pulled out. This added to my excitement, as the idea of hunting an elk paradise without competition was just too good to be true.

It was near the end of November and the beginning of a record cold spell. The temperature at the trailhead was minus 24 degrees, which would actually seem warm in a few days. It was interesting how comfortable the horses were in the cold, even though they had balls of ice in their tails and along their legs from repeated river-crossings. Elk had been spotted on previous rides into camp, so everyone kept their eyes on the open spots and I had my rifle ready. This time, the elk stayed in the timber.

Any doubts that the area held trophy elk were erased by the two massive racks lying next to the tack tent when we rode into camp. Taken just hours before, one later scored 376, won the Provincial Trophy and was also the best elk taken on a guided hunt by any outfitter member of the Rocky Mountain Elk Foundation that year. The other scored almost as well, even with a broken tine.

After that first cold and mostly sleepless night, someone was kind enough to start a fire in our tent terribly early the next morning, but we still had the pleasure of dressing in a frozen world. Even with the fire, the back end of the tent never got above freezing the entire trip. The temperature was minus 42 outside, and a howling wind chilled things down to about minus 80. Cold like that makes it hard to get excited about anything, but as always, the hunters were greeted with a warm breakfast, saddled horses and enthusiasm from the guides.

My first day was spent hunting Heartbreak Hill, and I could not have been happier. Tim, my guide, led me nearly straight up some 2,000 lung-busting feet to a ridgetop before it was light enough to glass. Looking across the Panther River, he quickly picked up three big bulls lying on a small bench, and I found a monster 7x7 working his way toward them. The big boy's antlers looked three times as wide as his back, but there was nothing we could do but watch. The river was simply too high and too fast to cross.

The cold we were fighting had slowed the elk migration to a trickle, but Tim hoped we could still pick up a bull coming out on our side of the river.

All we ended up with that day were frozen parts, yet watching all the elk and bighorn sheep made bearing the cold worthwhile. The camp was scoreless that day, but sleep came easy.

Plans were made the next morning to swing down the river, find a safe spot to cross and double back to try for the big seven. Tim thought it over and surprised me by suggesting that we go another direction on horseback. We saw several bulls that day as well, including one keeper that made it into the trees before we could close the distance. The other hunters struck out as well.

We saw elk every day of the trip, and I flat missed on my first opportunity. A wonderful old bull surprised us as we rounded a bend in the trail, and I made the rookie mistake of shooting before getting settled. My next chance was lost to twilight when the crosshairs blended into the coming darkness. The worst one happened after we spotted a big bull from just 200 yards. I reached for my rifle and accidentally opened the floorplate, wedging the rifle inside the scabbard. By the time I got it freed and a round stuffed into the chamber, the bull had walked out of sight. Things were not going my way.

The big bulls were invariably too far off and the cold balled up the migration that normally moved them through the area in good numbers. The guides, and particularly Clarence, tried harder every day, yet we always seemed to be on the wrong ridge. I turned down several bulls that I would have been happy to take anywhere else, waiting for something special.

The other hunters had better luck; five big bulls had been killed since I arrived at camp, all of them around 350. Sooner or later, I told myself, it would be my turn.

The last day of the season was clear and cold like the rest, but we saddled up and left with the encouragement of everyone in camp. As Clarence and I rode out, I couldn't say that I felt very confident, but he never seemed to waiver.

We spent two hours in the saddle without stopping before Clarence saw a lone bull skylined at the top of a hill. Through binoculars we could clearly count his points, but there was nothing for cover between us. It was all but impossible to be sure of his size. Still, he looked good and we figured him for my last chance.

I made my way through the timber alone, climbing to what looked like a good place for a shot. All I saw were tracks in the wind-blown snow where he had tried to scrape through, searching for food. Through the binoculars I followed his trail around the basin and found him there, peering over a ridge but well within range. All he had to do was take one step backward and he would be out of sight.

The slope where I was standing was steep so I fell sideways into the snow to get steady. It worked, and as he turned to go I hit him through the lungs. He took it hard but stayed up so I squeezed off again, but the cold caused a misfire. The next round did what it was supposed to do, and the bull went down.

It took me a long time to climb to where he lay, a good 7x7, but younger than I would have liked. Still, after nine hard days of temperatures under minus 20, no one on earth could have told me he was anything but a trophy. Clarence joined me, and together we tumbled the bull down to the horses. We quartered him as fast as we could and made it back to camp for a late lunch.

The area around Banff has produced some remarkable bulls over the years. Albertans can be proud of their elk herd, and combining the scenery with the trophy potential made me want to return. Sadly, regulations changed the following year and the area was put on strict quota. Outfitting rights were auctioned to the highest bidder. Several of us got together to help the Browns hold the area, but our bid came up short.

Every fall for the last 25 years I have thought about that camp, those huge elk and the great bunch of people who hunted them with me. I would give just about anything to do it again, no matter the cold.

Originally published in the Summer 1986 issue of Bugle *magazine.*

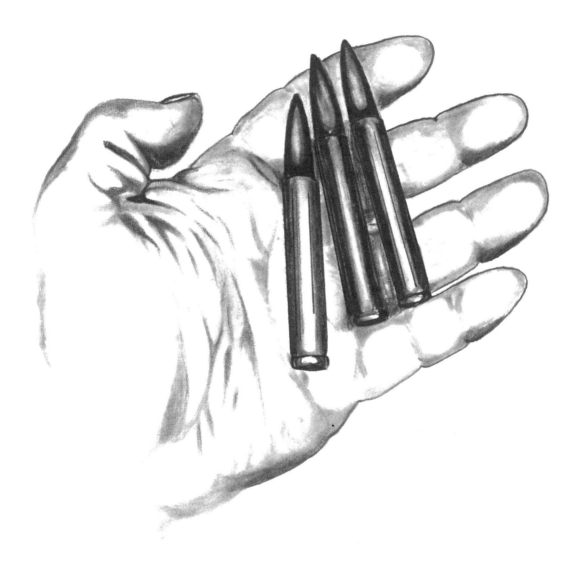

Jocelyn Russell
© 2009

Chapter 27

The Little Details

The chill of the house betrayed the intense cold outside, even for November. After adding some larch to the woodstove, I checked to see if my coat and hat were dry from yesterday's climb, then slipped them on. Shotgun, the highborn golden retriever who had appointed herself the guardian of my children, nudged at my leg and went to the door. I let her out, filled the Thermos with coffee and picked up my rifle. Shotgun was already waiting to come back inside. The snow had stopped, but several inches had stacked on the Jeep during the night and it started hard. I swept it off and wished for a garage.

I love to hunt alone. The high ridges, alpine meadows and cold wind of early winter have always been something of a vice. They have come together and drawn me from warm beds and away from family and fires for as long as I can remember. Although I go to the mountains at other times of the year, even to the same spots, being there as a hunter means something more. The heft of a rifle and the feel of heavy wool make it the place where I find my peace.

I hit the pavement, remembering to fasten the seatbelt and tap the brakes to check for ice. Then came a regimented mental inventory – clothing, pack, camera, flares, food, water, matches, rope and so on. It should all be there, and thinking about it helped the drive go faster. No tracks showed on the forest service road, so the mountain was all mine.

I stopped to lock in the hubs and shifted to 4-low before coming to the fork that climbed west toward the Idaho border. A little whitetail buck bounded down the road ahead, flagging his long tail. He looked like a projected slide in the glow of the headlights and reminded me that I had a deer tag in my pocket. But I was thinking about elk now, so I didn't pay him any mind.

Fresh snow at the trailhead was deeper than at home, but I was a couple thousand feet higher and expected there to be more. No wind. Silence. A storybook day to hunt.

My lookout was almost an hour away and I wanted to be there before daybreak. Never stopping for a rest, I made it just as glassing light arrived like it always does in the back half of November, slow and unsure. I set up the spotting scope and began searching the larger openings across the drainage for telltale shapes and movements. The day felt so right. Elk could be anywhere. All I had to do was find them.

The coming light brought detail to the basin, first a distinct horizon, then trees and finally bits and pieces of meadows. Soon limbs, stumps and trails crisscrossing the far ridges became clear. Objects that were promising at first did not become elk and the snow began again, at least on and off. Fog rose slowly in the distant valleys. Far away a shot rolled.

Then the elk came. A lone cow rose out of the ground and began pawing for food on a windswept slope. Another showed, and another, until there were nine. The bull following them stood a long time, just at the edge of the timber. He had strong eye guards, but that was all I could see through my binoculars. I rested the rifle across my backpack and twisted the Leupold scope up to 10-power. The intersection of the crosshairs was steady. The bull stood forever, it seemed, then slowly walked into the meadow.

I checked and rechecked the distance. No problem with this rifle, just pick a spot. He stopped again, and I strained to get a good look at his antlers. I already knew by the size of his frame that he was the best bull I had ever seen, but wanted to be sure. It seemed he was looking straight away for an eternity, then half-heartedly tossing an antler at a calf, he turned broadside. There – right behind the shoulder. I had him now and took one last look at his head. There was no fifth tine on the near side, so I pulled my finger away from the trigger. Missing or broken, I couldn't tell, but the point wasn't there.

The elk fed for a long time, but I kept watching, hoping the missing time would somehow grow back or that another bull would show up.

The Little Details

One by one, they eventually moved into the trees, the big bull following along behind. I was not tempted. This year it was trophy or nothing.

The wind began whispering out of the north when it was time for lunch. I decided to give my eyes a rest, retreated out of the basin and built a small fire on the other side. Sleepy, I managed a short nap.

Waking some minutes later, I checked my watch, confirming there was plenty of time to get back to the lookout. With a couple of hours to spare, I decided to explore a ridge I'd never climbed. Breaking out of the timber and following a sheep trail, I nearly ran over a bedded mule deer buck. We stared at each other for a second, then he exploded from his bed and bounded uphill in that stiff-legged gait of his kind. I briefly tracked him through the scope, more out of habit than anything else, because I knew he was not carrying a wide, heavy rack that would make packing him out worthwhile. Soon he intersected the sheep trail, slowed to a walk and crossed the ridge. I followed.

I sat at the top until the cold wind drove me back to the fire, now nothing more than a thin whisper of smoke. I pulled on the stiff coat, then the pack and hurried back to my stand. Twilight came quickly, shadows climbing the sides of the basin. I worked the glasses hard, searching again in all the likely places. Nothing came. Coyotes howled somewhere in the distance. An owl boomed, telling all who cared to listen that it was his turn to go hunting. I soon ran out of light, packed up and headed down along my morning's track. The clouds scattered and soft moonlight illuminated the path.

The trip down went all too quickly, and soon I was at the Jeep. I decided to sit on the bumper, enjoying the last granola bar and a cup of barely warm coffee. Finished, I returned to a nearby tree where I had rested the rifle. As I always do, I dropped the floorplate to empty the magazine into my hand. When I didn't feel the rounds drop or hear the clinking sound they make, I quickly worked the bolt only to find that the chamber, too, was empty.

It took a bit to realize I had forgotten to load the rifle. After pondering if it really mattered, I laughed out loud at myself, then drove home to my waiting family.

Originally published in the Spring 1991 issue of Bugle *magazine.*

Chapter 28

Above All Else

There were good reasons to climb the mountain. Even though it was mid-October, the weather was perfect. From the top, the fires of '88 could still be seen smoldering in Yellowstone Park 20 miles to the south. The view stretched beyond the Lee Metcalf Wilderness Area in every direction, one chain of ragged peaks after another rising from the Madison, Gallatin and Yellowstone valleys. Elk that lived in the lower elevations were heading back to their bedding areas after being up all night, alternately rutting and feeding. Panoramic views and elk aside, we had another reason to leave the comfortable camp below timberline and slowly climb tallus slopes to 10,000 feet. Somewhere up there was a tremendous mountain goat we had watched from camp, and I had a permit that said I could take him home – if I was lucky enough to find him.

From the time I was a boy I had dreamed of hunting one of these magnificent white beasts at the top of the world, but never thought I would have the chance because the permits were so difficult to draw. I tried for years when I lived in Washington and kept at it after moving to Montana. I couldn't believe my good luck when my wife called one August afternoon and told me she was holding the permit in her hand. I already knew who had to be my guide, a friend with the wonderful name of Merritt Pride.

Merritt operated the Lost Fork Ranch near the area I'd drawn and knew ever peak and cranny. For years he'd made his living guiding hunters and family vacation parties through Yellowstone and the surrounding areas. It was Merritt who had suggested I apply for this area, because it saw almost no goat-hunting pressure due to its inaccessibility.

I phoned Merritt and we decided on a mid-October hunt so the goats would have time to grow their winter coats. Just before we finished our conversation, I told him that I wanted to take my goat with a handgun, as it represented one of the supreme challenges in mountain hunting. Only a handful of people had done it. I promised myself not only to wait for a sure shot, but to hold out for a truly big goat.

Several weeks earlier I had received a Freedom Arms .454 Casull, a Field Grade model with adjustable sight and smooth black Micarta grips. To help tame recoil it was Mag-Na-Ported. Out-of-the-box accuracy was exceptional. Knowing I needed every advantage, I added a 2x Leupold scope. After several trips to the range, the Casull began to show its potential. The groups shrank until I could consistently put all five shots inside 2 inches at 100 yards. The Casull's performance certainly boosted my confidence and proved what a properly equipped, high-quality handgun can do.

Finally, it was time to leave for West Yellowstone and meet Merritt at his new lodge near the Madison River. After a short tour, we sat down to talk about goats and hunting them. Merritt has a degree in wildlife biology from Montana State and I knew that his expertise would prove invaluable.

The finest trophies are old males and the best way to determine the sex of a goat is to observe it for a time and note its urination posture. Both horn length and body size can be deceiving to the untrained eye. The male's horns are thicker and have more of a curve than those of a nanny. In general, if the bases appear thick and close together, it's a billy. If the horns appear tall and straight, it's a nanny.

Mature males are generally loners, while females are often seen in the company of other goats or their young. The coat of a mature billy often has a yellowish cast from wallowing in rutting pits scratched out at the edge of feeding areas. They're also larger through the chest and shoulders than a nanny, but as the winter coat develops this characteristic can be misleading. On the adults of both sexes, the beard extends the full length of the face, while a juvenile's beard is less prominent.

The horns grow from a bony core and usually reach maximum size by the time the animal is 3 years old. Like wild sheep, a mountain goat's age can be determined by counting the number of rings in the horns. Males with horns exceeding 10 inches are taken in the best areas of Washington, Canada and Alaska, but a 9-inch billy with 5 inches of circumference is considered a trophy in just about any area of Montana.

Early the next morning we loaded up the horses and mules and drove to the trailhead at the southern end of the Lee Metcalf. Even at 6,000 feet it was shirt-sleeve weather. I was concerned the goats might not have grown their winter coats, but Merritt felt sure we'd find them with 5 or 6 inches of guard-hair over their fine inner wool.

We had ridden several hours before the first ragged cliffs came into sight. One minute we were in elk summer range, the next approaching some of the most rugged country I'd ever seen. The basins at first narrowed then abruptly ended, climbing thousands of feet from timberline. The steep slopes were mostly broken granite patchworked with stands of wind-battered limber pine and dwarf alpine fir. As we climbed, small areas of grass began to appear far up on the slopes, poking through where the rocks thinned. These were the small patches where the goats fed.

Camp was already set for our arrival, and what a camp it was. Situated on the shoreline of one of the many lakes in the area, it blended in so well with the surrounding trees I didn't see it until we were next to a tent. After unloading, we decided to do some glassing, so we headed up to a ridge that offered a commanding view of the entire drainage.

As the shadows began to creep up the distant peaks we saw our first goat. Merritt found him through his spotting scope, and I quickly switched from binoculars to my 25x Leupold and focused in on him. He was over a mile away, feeding near the top. We were fighting an evening wind that jostled the scopes just enough to make judging the horns difficult, but there was no doubt it was a billy. His shiny, ebony-colored horns had a distinct hook, and his yellow coat and shoulder hump made him appear much blockier than I had expected. Merritt felt it was the big billy he'd watched through the summer and asked if I wanted to get closer. Reluctantly, I decided to pass since I was curious to see what else was in the area.

As Merritt continued watching the billy, I switched back to the binoculars and began to look for others. I spotted a nanny with her kid feeding in an avalanche chute. They were soon joined by another pair that had been bedded behind some rocks, and I realized how much smaller they were than the billy. I switched back to the spotting scope just in time to see him walk out of sight. I told Merritt how big he seemed compared to the others, and he quickly confirmed that it was a billy, with horns of at least 9 inches.

The next morning we were glassing at first light. We both focused on the spot where we'd seen the billy, hoping he had not wandered too far. We finally spotted him and watched for an hour, all the while carefully planning our stalk and waiting for him to bed. After he did, we picked a route and some landmarks, realizing that as soon as we moved he would be out of sight. We stopped at camp for extra water, then started to climb.

At first the going was easy, but once above timberline we had to cross steep chutes and sharp ridges. To keep the wind in our favor, we had to approach from below. As we neared the crest of the ridge where we would begin our final stalk, we paused for a drink and I thumbed five rounds into the pistol. I could tell that Merritt was excited. He knew the goat was big and wanted to make sure we got as close as possible.

The wind was right and we slowly crept up the ridge. We hadn't gone far when Merritt hit the ground and motioned me to follow. I threw off my pack and quickly crawled up to join him, but it was too late. The goat had bolted from his bed. I never saw him, but the look on Merritt's face told me he was big. We backtracked down the mountain and finally stopped to talk.

Merritt chose his words carefully. He estimated the goat's horns at 9 inches, maybe more. He wanted to make sure and get another look if he could, however, because the billy had turned and ran so quickly. If we didn't press him, Merritt reasoned, he might stop at the head of the drainage and give us another chance.

We rested for nearly two hours, admiring the panorama, nervously making small talk and enjoying the warmth of the autumn sun. The goat had headed toward an extremely rugged area where he would be difficult to approach within handgun distance and where he could fall

216

several hundred feet if I didn't stop him quickly. Or, he might have continued through that area, which meant we would probably never see him again. I tried not to think about that.

When it was time to go, I checked the pistol one last time, then we pulled on our packs and climbed up the ridge past the place where we'd spooked him.

We walked slowly, each concentrating on one side of the sharp, narrow ridge. As we neared the head of the drainage, Merritt whispered that unless the billy had run down the side of the mountain he had to be very close, as a steep drop was just ahead. He took one more step and then grabbed my arm hard, nearly tearing me off my feet. The big billy was bedded just 60 yards ahead, facing in the other direction.

I drew the Casull and crept forward, Merritt's hand on my elbow. Slowly the goat came into view. His long, white coat rippled in the mountain breeze and the tips of his horns looked like daggers sticking above his back. I slowly went to a knee and thumbed the hammer.

The billy must have heard the cylinder rotate and lock. In an instant he turned his head, saw us and exploded out of his bed. Merritt shouted for me to take him and I squeezed off a shot. The 260-grain flat-point slammed into his ribs just behind the shoulder, but didn't draw the slightest reaction. As he headed for a point that dropped down to rocks hundreds of feet below, I put two more rounds right behind the first, then another high into his shoulder that should have caught his spine and brought him down.

My final shot raked him from the rear of his ribs through the off shoulder, but he still showed no sign of letting up. He ran right to the edge of the drop and stood there, head hanging. If he had taken another step or fallen forward, he would have broken his horns to bits on the rocks below. Frantically, I unloaded the cylinder and tore open the cartridge carrier on my belt for fresh rounds.

It seemed to take forever to load the pistol, but I was trying to keep an eye on the goat. As I frantically thumbed cartridges into the cylinder, he began to wobble, then slowly lowered his head and fell backward into a little chute where he rolled several times before hanging up on a clump of grass. Merritt let out a war cry loud enough to stampede the bison in West Yellowstone. It was all I could do to put the pistol back in the holster and shake his outstretched hand.

We hurriedly gathered our gear and made our way down the chute to the billy. When we got to him, we were relieved to see that his coat was in prime condition and that his heavy horns were over 9 inches long, though one tip had been chipped when he fell. We took pictures and then skinned him for a full mount, working fast so we would not be caught on the mountain after dark.

We pulled camp and hit the trail the next morning. Except for a brief mule rodeo that launched the goat's cape high into the air and cost us an hour of repacking, we had a great trip out. After helping Merritt unload, I drove home with the beautiful horns resting on the seat beside me, eager to show them to my family.

Not long after I had the horns measured by Duncan Gilchrest, an expert on mountain goats, and learned that my billy tied the handgun world record. Duncan seemed even more excited than I was upon making that discovery.

Now, almost two decades after packing that goat down the mountain, he remains one of my favorite trophies. Each year I put in for another permit, and I hope to get lucky enough to have another chance before the mountains get too tall to climb.

Originally published as "White Spot on the Mountain" in the August 1990 issue of Petersen's Hunting Magazine. *Published as "Above All Else" in the May/June 2009 issue of* Sporting Classics.